W9-BNG-533

LIBRARY OF
JSL
JAMES LLOYD

NAUTICAL QUARTERLY

Dear Nautical Quarterly Reader:

We take special pride in the photographs we publish, and this issue brings together some of the best marine photography we have had the pleasure of bringing you during four years of publishing. Marine photography is a demanding discipline--light on the water is brighter than land light on a sunny day, and exposures are more difficult to control; on a grey day subtleties of color and image are there but it takes a skilled photographer to get them. On some assignments the action is split-second; on others the photographer will be alert for hours to find or anticipate a great image. On-the-water photographs like these represent not only artistry but hard work.

The photos we bring you here have a nice variety, too--the wet, gritty realism of Eric Poggenpohl's coverage of the Chesapeake oyster dredgers; the equally wet but high-spirited images of Hobie Cat sailing and socializing from Chris Cunningham; Joe Upton's moody photographs of Pacific fishing; the little boat from the Adirondacks that Jim Brown has captured while also capturing the very spirit of summertime sailing; the Eric Schweikardt photographs of everything from big-boat ocean racing to a Cigarette raceboat at speed.

Readers who come by for a chat during boat shows never fail to tell us how much pleasure they get from photographs like these. We take equal pleasure--and great pride--in bringing them to you issue after issue.

Cordially,

Donald C. McGraw, Jr.
Publisher

LIBRARY OF ... LLOYD

373 PARK AVENUE SOUTH, NEW YORK, NEW YORK 10016 TELEPHONE: (212) 689-8232

TABLE OF CONTENTS

AUTUMN 1981 **NAUTICAL QUARTERLY** AUTUMN 1981

PUBLISHER: DONALD C. McGRAW, JR.
EDITOR: JOSEPH GRIBBINS
CREATIVE DIRECTOR: B. MARTIN PEDERSEN
DESIGN FIRM: JONSON/PEDERSEN/ HINRICHS & SHAKERY, INC.

MANAGING EDITOR: MICHAEL LEVITT
ASSOCIATE EDITOR: REBECCA SMITH
ASSISTANT ART DIRECTOR: RANDELL PEARSON
DESIGN ASSISTANT: RODERICK B. WARD
STAFF PHOTOGRAPHER: ALLAN WEITZ

MANAGING DIRECTOR: C.S. LOVELACE
CIRCULATION DIRECTOR: DAVID B. WALLACE
CIRCULATION MANAGER: ELISSA deBRITO
OFFICE MANAGER: LIZ MONTALVO
SPECIAL PROJECTS: ANDREW McCOLOUGH
ASSISTANT TO THE PUBLISHER: MIRANDA SCHILLER

CONTRIBUTING EDITORS:
EDWIN OSBORNE/THE WEST COAST
ANGUS LENNOX/THE U.K.
ANNICA DAHLSTROM/SCANDINAVIA
MAXIM GOLIARD/THE CONTINENT
JONATHAN WONG/THE FAR EAST

NAUTICAL QUARTERLY IS PUBLISHED IN WINTER, SPRING, SUMMER AND FALL BY NAUTICAL QUARTERLY, INC., 373 PARK AVENUE SOUTH, NEW YORK, N.Y. 10016. COPYRIGHT ©1981 NAUTICAL QUARTERLY, INC.: ALL RIGHTS RESERVED UNDER PAN AMERICAN AND UNIVERSAL COPYRIGHT CONVENTIONS; REPRODUCTION WITHOUT PERMISSION IS PROHIBITED. EDITORIAL SUBMISSIONS SHOULD BE SENT TO THE ADDRESS ABOVE, AND SHOULD BE ACCOMPANIED BY A SELF-ADDRESSED, STAMPED ENVELOPE. WE WILL ACCEPT NO RESPONSIBILITY, HOWEVER, FOR UNSOLICITED GRAPHIC OR EDITORIAL MATERIAL. ON EDITORIAL MATTERS, PHONE 212-685-9114. SUBSCRIPTION CORRESPONDENCE, BOOKSTORE ORDERS AND ORDERS FOR BACK COPIES SHOULD BE SENT TO THE ADDRESS ABOVE, OR BY PHONE TO 212-685-9114. U.S. AND CANADIAN SUBSCRIPTIONS ARE $49.50 PER YEAR. ALL OTHERS ARE $55 (U.S.), EXCEPT AUSTRALIA AND NEW ZEALAND AT $80 (A or N.Z.) FROM DAVID BATEMAN LTD., BOX 65062, MAIRANGI BAY, AUCKLAND 10, N.Z. FOREIGN SUBSCRIBERS ARE SERVED ONLY BY SURFACE MAIL. SECOND-CLASS POSTAGE FOR NAUTICAL QUARTERLY 15 (ISSN 0199-0837) IS PAID AT NEW YORK, N.Y. AND AT ADDITIONAL MAILING OFFICES.

ARSTER DRUDGIN'

WINTER & SPRING

BY RANDALL PEFFER
PHOTOS BY ERIC POGGENPOHL

10
RUBY G FORD

Oyster season opened. On a sunless morning twenty skipjacks nodded their bowsprits over the currents of Knapps Narrows and the shadows of Dogwood Cove. The oyster sloops groaned in gusts of snow. Halyards slapped rapidly on the masts. The wind blew out of the west at twenty knots. Even if the snow kept up, I knew we would leave port: this was the weather Tilghman Islanders called a "drudger's breeze." □ *Ruby Ford* pitched among the pack of similar dredge boats. Although she was the oldest skipjack in the fleet, she lacked none of the grace of the younger boats (most of which were built between 1900 and 1925). Her long clipper bow, raked mast, low-slung white hull, and push boat swaying astern on davits disguised the *Ruby G. Ford*'s broad fifteen-foot deck. Like a barge her flat bottom drew only three and a half feet of water with the centerboard up. Yet *Ruby Ford* had the character of a tall ship: mast hoops, leg-o'-mutton rig, manila lines, cotton jib, spiderweb-like lazyjack lines on the club jib and main boom, enough wooden blocks to make an antique dealer drool, and a Richardson steering wheel dated 1889.

"Where we drudgin' today?"
"River," said Murphy in a way that made it plain
he resented being questioned . . .

After less than a week's work, *Ruby Ford* looked worn to me. Not only was her paint chipped and rust-streaked from weather and work, but her deck looked like a junkyard. The large gasoline engine and winding machine gears amidship were the guts of the dredging operation. Six man-sized iron and net cages that were the oyster dredges leaned against the mast, the winding machine housing, and each other. That was just the beginning. Shovels, open oil drums, buckets, sawhorses, air-cooled bilge pumps, propane gas containers, boxes full of rusty fittings, tools, tarps, oilskins, and what seemed dozens of rubber gloves were scattered over the boat. Everything was streaked with gray mud and bits of oyster shells.

I walked up and down the wharf to keep warm. After several minutes I heard a pickup truck bang up the road over frozen ruts and lurch to a stop. Three men jumped out of the back and two more piled from the cab—*Ruby Ford*'s crew. They shuffled along the wharf awkwardly in thermal underwear, jeans, layers of sweaters, parkas, and hip boots. Crews stirred on other boats. They complained. Their skipjacks were from "down Bay," and they lived aboard in the forecastles while their boats were working the rich oyster beds off Tilghman Island. From the complaints voiced by some of the down-Bay watermen, it seemed that *Ruby Ford*'s crew wasn't missing much of the romance by living at home.

We boarded the vessel. No one spoke. The cook went below deck and sent a yellow light shining from the cabin companionway across the steering wheel of the *Ruby Ford*. Bart Murphy busied himself priming a gasoline bilge pump. Bobby and I opened the hatch over the oyster hold and checked the water level in the bilges. *Ruby Ford* had taken on eight inches of water during the night. We lowered the siphon hose into the bilge. The captain started the pump.

Bobby and I joined the cook and the rest of the crew. In *Ruby Ford*'s cabin the watermen seemed jammed into a boat a quarter of a skipjack's size. There was no passageway leading through the forward bulkhead. What made my claustrophobia worse was the way the bulkhead was lined with shelving containing more coffee-making materials than a diner. A propane gas stove hissed almost in center cabin, and the six of us huddled together in the eight-by-eight room. There was not quite standing headroom. I sat on a quarter berth (a fourteen-inch plank). Behind it I could see spare parts stashed in the bilges: plank and spare timber, life jackets, old lines, discarded pots and pans, lots of undiscernible pieces of metal, and oilskins and rubber gloves. *Ruby Ford* stank—kerosene, coffee, bacon, eggs, toast, grits, and humanity. The crew drank coffee and ate. They joked and sniped at each other. The two whites and two older blacks traded racial jests. I tried to laugh at the appropriate times.

Where was the captain? Off trying to decide where to go "drudgin'."

The crew tried to second-guess their captain, but after much speculation as to where the *Ruby Ford* would work today they admitted that they did this every morning and were always wrong. One of the men cursed the early hour. Another cursed the weather. Then the Bay. Then the crew. Then the boat. The cursing stopped. The watermen seemed to know they had gone too far; they changed the subject.

Bobby teased the black cook; "You marry that old lady of yours yet, Bernard?"

"Shit, no. I too smart and too young for that. I seen what marriage do for you. Get your white ass in one goddamn sling . . ."

A pair of boots attached to a muddy blue insulated suit dropped through the companionway—Bart Murphy. The jibes ceased and the question was asked, "Where we drudgin' today?"

"River," said Murphy in a way that made it plain that he resented being questioned by the crew.

The smiles disappeared from the crew's faces, and the conversation turned more serious. This was a matter of money. The captain wouldn't go

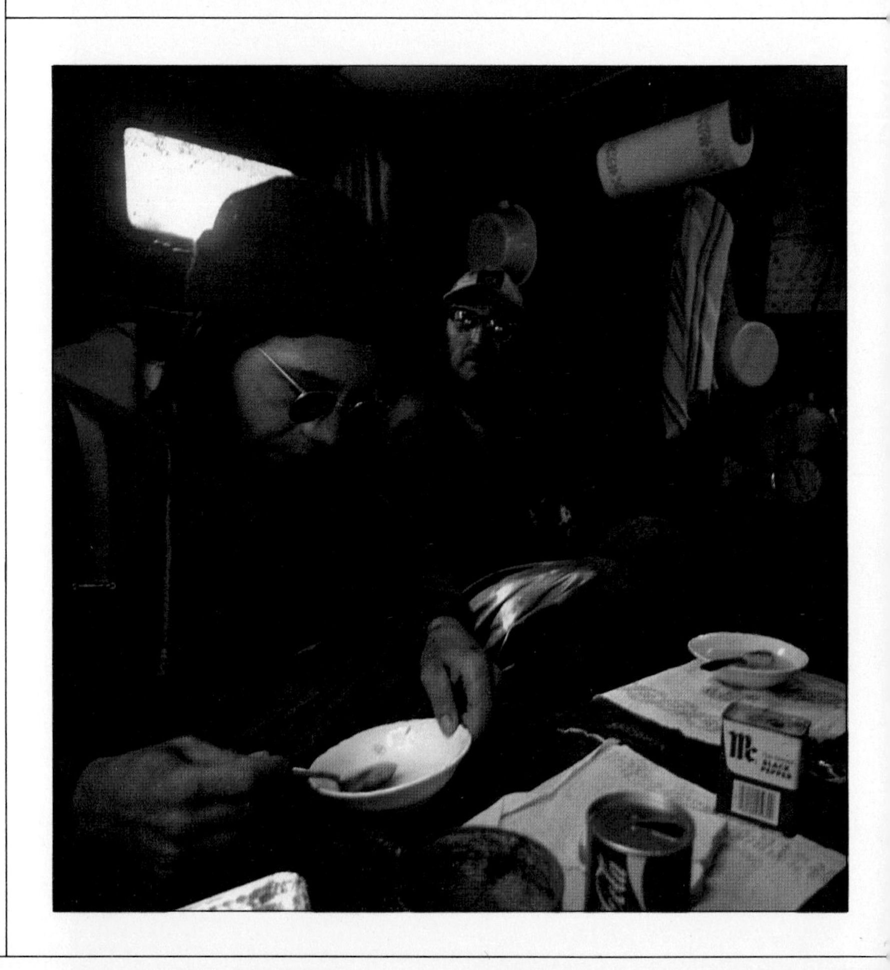

Someone said it was going to be "a long mother of a day." Heave. Ho. Ice built up on deck.

out in the Bay because it was too rough for dredging. Today they would work the oyster bed on the eastern side of Tilghman Island in the mouth of the Choptank River where the water was "ca'm." The oysters from the river would bring only about three dollars a bushel. Oysters from the Bay might earn six dollars.

The crew talked about the economics of the boat. During the winter season the skipjacks try to work Monday through Friday if their buyers have a market, and if the weather permits. Each workday the boat's earnings are divided into shares. One-third of the total covers the boat's needs for food, fuel, sails, rigging, planking, engines, paint, and haulout—a figure that often exceeds $10,000 a year. The remaining profits are divided equally among the captain and the five crewmen. When the boat catches its limit of 150 bushels of six-dollar oysters, a man can make $100 a day, but the average earnings are far below that. Skipjack crewmen might make $5,000 in a season. All of them "go crabbin'" during the summer. They didn't much need days like this.

Bart Murphy finished his coffee and we followed him on deck to get the *Ruby Ford* underway. A three-knot current rushed past the wharf where she tied up in Knapps Narrows. *Ruby Ford* needed to turn 180 degrees, bow into the current, in order to head east to the oysterbeds. We paid out line to lower the push boat. Then we harnessed its nose into a notch on the starboard side of the skipjack's stern. Bobby swung into the push boat and idled its V-8. The crew tried to let the current swing *Ruby Ford*'s stern around, but the bowsprit snagged on the skipjack moored inboard. For twenty minutes we pushed, pulled, and swore at the bowsprit until we sprang free of the *Seagull*.

The push boat drove *Ruby Ford* under the drawbridge that connects Tilghman Island with Bay Hundred Peninsula. We found open water. The sun hadn't come up yet, and my rubber gloves were damp from line handling. They began to freeze. It continued to snow.

We kept warm by breaking out the mud dredges (different kinds of dredges for different bottoms) and rigging them to steel cables on the winding machine. At the captain's command everyone grabbed the main halyard and heaved 1200 square feet of new dacron (the first synthetic sail the *Ruby Ford* has ever had) aloft, leaving four reefs tucked in the sail. There was no winch to stretch out the halyard—snub it, cleat it.

Astern sixteen other skipjacks worked their way out into three-foot seas. We shut down the push boat and hauled it aboard. I waited for the moment of screeching gulls, splattering waves across the bow, the snapping dacron, and the command that would bring them all to the sheets to trim sail. It never came.

Ruby Ford nodded off the wind and trimmed up untended on a beam reach. The source of this surprise: Bart Murphy had knotted the main sheet to the traveler in such a way that it appeared that this point of sail had been trimmed into the *Ruby Ford* for the season.

The dredgeboat slopped through the snow flurries at about three knots. She could take more sail. Bart Murphy felt it and called forward to pull up the shortened jib. The head sail trimmed stiff without anyone's touching a sheet.

Bart pushed a switch and the winder engine, a six-cylinder Chevy, began to cough and bang. The captain yelled "heave" and the crew chorused "ho" as we slipped the two dredges over the sides. The dredge cable creaked over the rollers amidship until the dredges began raking over the bottom.

It had been this way since 1865. That year Maryland lifted a prohibition on dredging, which had been outlawed since 1820 because it threatened to rake the upper Chesapeake clean of oysters. Lifting the ban on dredging was the Maryland legislature's reaction to political pressure from oystermen who could only harvest oysters through the slow, laborious method of plucking them from the bottom with tongs. They complained that the ban placed them in a weak position to compete in the marketplace

"What you know. You jus' too goddamn dumb to worry. I dredged for arsters 'fore you was born..."

with Virginia watermen who were permitted to dredge the lower Chesapeake. Even though Maryland's new dredging law attempted to regulate the oyster harvest through limiting dredging to sailboats working on designated bars, the efficient combination of dredge and skipjack increased the Chesapeake's annual yield of oysters in the years from 1865 to 1885 from 1,000,000 to 15,000,000 bushels. After 1885 the harvest shrunk dramatically due to overfishing with the efficient dredge. However, the skipjack and dredge were here to stay. Cull law and daily limits have to save the Chesapeake oyster from extinction. In the 1977–78 season Maryland oystermen harvested 2,290,802 bushels, an average catch by the standards of the last twenty years.

As I waited for *Ruby Ford*'s dredges to fill with oysters, three skipjacks dragged dangerously close across our vessel's bow. No one seemed to notice. We were called to work by the captain speeding up the winder engine. This was his signal to us to engage the winder clutches and reel aboard the oyster dredges.

The dredge frames banged up over the rails. Two men worked each dredge. We swung the pocket-like net bag up over the side and emptied fifty pounds of muddy shells on the work deck just aft of the mast. Bart Murphy brought *Ruby Ford* about and hollered forward "heave." We sang "ho" and let the dredges slide the three fathoms back to the bottom.

Ruby Ford needed all her crew: two or three men bent spread-legged over each pile of dredgings. We culled good oysters from the piles and scooped them between our legs like dogs digging holes. Some crabs crawled among the debris. We tossed them into a spare dredge for safe-keeping (dinner). The rest of the first dredging—probably 70 percent of what we had pulled up—was refuse (old oyster shells, bottles, and beer cans). We shoveled it over the side. Someone said it was going to be "a long mother of a day." Heave, ho.

Ice built up on deck. There were no life lines, and I began to worry about working the dredge on the leeward side of the boat. It would be easy to fall overboard. Bobby and Bernard kneeled beside me culling oysters. Waves rushed regularly over the bulwark and around our legs. Each wave left more ice.

Bernard swore: "Fuck this shit. Goddamn captain goin' to drown me."

"You're just a chickenshit nigger, it's all you are, Bernard," said Bobby. "Ain't this little bit o' water, or Bart, goin' to hurt you either bit."

"What you know. You jus' too goddamn dumb to worry. I dredged for arsters 'fore you was born, and I seen all the dead niggers that washed up on this friggin' shore come drudgin' season. Some o' them old captains throw'd niggers overboard for fun. This ain't goddamn bath water, you know."

"Chickenshit. What in God's good name am I doin' workin' with this yellow-ass nigger?" Bobby shook his head in disbelief.

"Hell, no" said several voices.
"Let's see how it goes." "We out here, now."
"May as well work."

"Goddamn, boy. I'm tellin' you it's only the fool ain't scared o' this Bay. I seen a man get overboard in this weather. Workin' the lee drudge just like this. We's haulin' the drudge and its ice. Wham. He slips. The drudge has thrown that man overboard. In seconds we throws two life rings to him, but he don't even swim for 'em—and he could swim—he just drown. Never found the body. This the worst fuckin' work. You think they call it "drudgin'" cause it's so much fun? Fuck this shit..."

The routine continued. By 9:30 the snow had stopped. Yet more than twelve skipjacks hauled dredges and ran for home. The chill factor was below zero. Bobby said the other crews were chickenshits. Only two other boats continued to work. Bart Murphy paced the deck in front of the steering wheel, kicking the cabin side and hugging his shoulders to keep warm. He figured he owed the crew a conference; we had only caught about fifteen bushels of oysters.

Ruby Ford held her footing while Bart came forward from his perch at the wheel and met the crew on the working deck. Go in?

"Hell, no" said several voices. "Let's see how it goes."

"We out here, now," said Bernard. "May as well work."

The men's decision was surprising to me. For an hour I had been daydreaming about my warm rented house on Tilghman's harbor. The crew seemed too independent to want to freeze their butts off for so few oysters. But the jibes the crew had taken at the captain as they worked were misleading; they had made him seem someone to be endured like Ahab. The complaints masked respect and affection. They said Bart had a plan, and they were with him.

The crew of the *Ruby Ford* hauled dredges, shook out two reefs, and sailed three miles to different oyster beds. The first haul produced oysters the size of grapefruit. Not high quality, but a good number of "keepers." The clouds had blown away, and we were left with a bright crisp day that almost made me forget how cold it was. Bart Murphy tossed his Clorox bottle buoy overboard. Bernard brewed coffee and the crew toasted a better day.

The *Ruby Ford* dredged into the afternoon that way—sailing and resailing half-mile tacks past the Clorox bottle. Haul, heave, cull, shovel; haul, heave, cull, shovel. Thirty, fifty, eighty bushels of oysters and talk to pass the time.

The crew told stories about Vietnamese girls, guns, and boats and Eastern Shore girls, guns, and boats.

"See that old drudge boat layin' over in them shallows," said Bernard pointing to a wreck near Tilghman Island. "She had one right smart captain, you know. Boat was old and small—not much to speak of. Wouldn't catch her limit. So I guess her captain got tired o' bein' poor. 'Fuck it,' he say, and when no one is lookin' he runs the old tub ashore and fixes an illegal propeller in her. Smart? I'm tellin' you. He rigged that

"Somebody try to save an
old wreck like that and make it a pleasure boat
.... These yachtsmen are crazy bastards."

propeller to run off the goddamn winder motor.

"Well pretty soon that old boat begins catchin' her limit every day. She's makin' money even when there weren't hardly no sailin' breeze. 'Course she running on the propeller. The sails is just up for decoration. But the captain he ain't lettin' on cause he knows some son of a bitch might get jealous, pissed off, and shoot him. Crew? Them niggers ain't sayin' nothin' 'bout the propeller 'cause they all gettin' rich.

"But that bunch of fools gets too greedy. They be racin' that drudge boat along at ten knots every time they think no one's goin' to see 'em. Now, you know the Marine Police is dumb, but you can only fuck 'em so long in the same way before it dawns on to 'em that they's gettin' screwed. So, in this case, it dawns on to 'em and they set up a sting.

"Here's how folks tell it. The drudgers out workin' the river. It's slick ca'm. The sails is just kinda hangin' loose from the mast and that propeller just movin' the boat real pretty. And they got on some arsters, too. Them niggers is singin' cause they makin' so much money. The police, they hidin' in the cove watchin' all this through binoculars. Hell, I think they might even been takin' pictures of this boat power drudgin'.

"When the police got this all documented, they came out of the cove with the lights flashin' and the siren wailin' on their old cruiser. Well, when the drudger sees this he knowed he's in trouble. So he says the hell with it and cranks up that propeller fast as she'll go. Heads right across the flats where the cruiser can't. Runs that skipjack right up close to shore till she sticks in the mud right where she's laying now. Then the captain and the niggers wade ashore. They is long gone from Tilghman Island 'fore the police ever get back to harbor.

"That old drudge boat weren't worth much anyway. But the Department of Natural Resources revoked her license, so she ain't no good to nobody. So there she sits—one fast boat... for a while."

"That never happens now," said Bobby, "Somebody try to save an old wreck like that and make it a pleasure boat. I ain't shittin' ya. These yachtsmen are crazy bastards."

What followed was a commentary by Bobby on the foolishness of yachtsmen. He told how Buck Garvin, the buyer for *Ruby Ford*'s catch, got calls every week asking if he knew where there was an old dredge boat someone could make into a yacht. Bobby laughed at the idea. He knew how uncomfortable it is to live on a skipjack, and he knew that any dredge boat a waterman wants to sell must not have a solid timber in her. But according to Bobby the yachtsmen don't seem to mind: he knew of one dredge boat a pleasure sailor bought without a marine survey—that didn't matter, but the man wouldn't hand over a nickel to the former skipper until he received a written history of the boat. The antique business is good on the Eastern Shore said Bobby.

Now, finding a dredge boat to work was difficult. Bart Murphy salvaged the *Ruby G. Ford* in 1972 after she had slipped a mooring, sunk two tonging boats, lost her push boat and bowsprit, and snagged on a bar in the Choptank River. Bart had sold his first skipjack and tried tonging for oysters. But he didn't like it, and he was looking for a way to get back into dredging. By rescuing the *Ruby Ford* he avoided months of searching and haggling with other watermen who might want to give up their skipjacks. Bart was so excited the day he finished repairing *Ruby Ford* that he didn't wait to find a crew—he took his new boat dredging and caught fourteen bushels of oysters single-handedly.

The mounds of oysters rested fore and aft on both sides of the boat. If *Ruby Ford* had her 150-bushel limit the mounds would be as large as the plywood sheets braced against the rails to prevent the oysters from falling overboard. The piles weren't that big. Bernard went below to make coffee. The rest of us sought out fresh sets of rubber gloves, warmed in the boat's oven. We were the last crew out by two hours. Now it was four o'clock and time to get home while there was light.

With sails furled the *Ruby G. Ford* tied along the buyer's wharf, and a crane with a steel bushel-bucket unloaded and tallied the catch. One hundred seven bushels. Bart Murphy went to collect the money.

We rinsed down the deck and hauled the push boat aboard. I listened to Bart and Bobby talk about crashing the bars in St. Michaels—"Honey, don't it seem time they let us back in there?"

The wind died, and the sun felt warm on my cheeks. Someone joked, "Wonder if tongin's this easy?"

"Believe 'tis," said Bobby, "but social life ain't nothin'."

"Heard that old man was dyin'.
What's that son of a bitch doin' runnin' our
boat?" asked Charlie Buck.

SPRING

During the final days of spatting in April the crew of *Ruby Ford* had taken to avoiding the cabin of the vessel. In the early sunrises of spring the work deck became the place where the crew would stretch out, make pillows of their oilskins, and sleep while the mate guided their skipjack on the hour and a half run to the spat beds. Below decks the stove remained fireless until calls for coffee sent Bernard down into the cabin to brew a "wake up" for the hands. Breakfast was a bologna and cheese sandwich just before adding oil and cranking over the winding machine.

It was on the last of those mornings of the winter/spring transition that the crew woke on deck with a start. Bernard was shaking them.

"Rise your asses, boys; I see we got trouble now."

"What's the matter, Bernard? You so tired from tomcattin' all night you ain't found the coffee yet?" asked Charlie Buck.

"You ain't seen tired yet. Look! Look what's cap'nin' this boat."

The men tried to focus on the figure at the wheel. It was not the thick form of the mate, Bobby. The helmsman was skinny and twisted. Black oilskin overalls and a red plaid shirt buttoned at the neck draped the man's bones. He leaned on the wheel from behind with both arms. The head thrust forward on the shoulders. Silver stubble covered the face.

"God," whispered one of the men. "Who's that?"

"If you're asking Bernard, I say it's the devil himself."

"Heard that old man was dyin'. What's that son of a bitch doin' runnin' our boat?" asked Charlie Buck.

"Why don't you ask him? See what that old bastard gives you."

"Give your black ass the heave ho. That's what."

" 'Deed he will. Just call me one shy nigger today. Watch me hide." Bernard pulled the brim of his sou'wester hat down over his eyes.

"Where'd that old man come from? Where's Bobby?" The crewmen pursued the conversation.

"Must o' been stowed away in the cabin. Damn, Bernard, why didn't you check 'fore we cast off? This white man would have stayed ashore if I know'd that crazy old man was cap'n."

"Lord, I'd a jumped ship with you. They say he ain't never been all together, if you know what I mean."

"Loony: rammed the *Ida Marshall* when she wouldn't break tacks with him. Yes sir, he sunk her. 'Swim home, you chickenshits,' he told her crew."

"That ain't the half of it."

"Say he used to get his crews over to Bal'mer. Shanghai'd 'em, that's what. Drug men aboard when they was stone drunk and left port. Told 'em: 'Cull oysters or swim.' "

"Couldn't get crew no other way."

"Well, goddamn Bart, and damn the mate: they fixed us now."

As the men talked they pretended to be greasing the winding machine. The conversation confirmed what I had suspected: the man at the helm was a retired skipjack captain. He had not sailed regularly for more than fifteen years, but he occasionally appeared without warning at the helm of one or another Tilghman skipjack. It was never clear whether the old captain was pressed into service by skippers or mates who wanted a day away from dredging, or whether the ancient skipper had driven the skipjacks' proper managers from the vessels' wheels through trickery or intimidation. The men on the *Ruby Ford* never mentioned the helmsman's proper name. Behind his back they called him the "old man" or "old bastard"; to his face they addressed him as "captain" and "sir." The crew accused the old man of everything from piracy to murder. It was common belief that the old man lived in a perpetual rage brought on by endless sipping on pints of rum. No one on Tilghman wanted to cross the old man, and everyone said there was never another captain who could catch more oysters or break a young man's spirit the way the *Ruby Ford*'s present skipper could. A hot old man. Full of riddles . . .

"Heave up the goddamn canvas. You boys think you're niggers at a watermelon picnic or what? Get to them sails. They'll be no pushin' for arsters while I'm cap'n. Get that push boat hauled out, Bobby." The old man's command sent the sails aloft and produced the mate who had been stationed in the push boat.

The crew lined the stern of *Ruby Ford* to haul the push boat out of the Bay, and their mate shrugged subtly to his friends as if to apologize for the old man's appearance. When the crew moved back to the work deck to break out the dredges the mate muttered: "He snuck up on me when we was a mile beyond the Narrows. Called me ten times the tail end of a mule. Got me into the push boat 'fore I knew whether to strike him or say a prayer. Coming a foul o' that old man has turned me inside out. Things is right queer. And he's queerest of all."

"Tend them sheets or you'll be walkin' home from here." The old man pointed to a slight shudder of cloth near the top of the sail, "She ain't right yet. Don't try and think about sailin.' Jus' pull on them sheets till I tell you to stop. Goin' to show these poor-excuse-for-watermen the right way to catch seed arsters. Damn 'em too if they don't make way." The old man raised his arm and gave the finger to six other skipjacks that were powering in circles over the spat bar.

"Heave them drudges."

"Ho."

The *Ruby Ford* cut across the bow of another skipjack. In the fifteen-knot breeze the sailboat raked oysters from the bottom in swift, graceful strokes. She seemed to move better than the boats under power. They

10

"He's just balls. That's the end on it. More juice than them prize bulls they got up the road."

rolled and pitched in the waves; *Ruby Ford*'s sails pulled her forward through the seas on a steady angle of heel.

"Don't that looney make her move some!" grinned Bernard as he helped to heave the starboard dredge into the Bay.

"Slack the jib sheet," called the captain. "Let them dredges out seven more feet. Shove them arsters up to the bow. This boat ain't sailin' square."

"Damn. Hear them orders. Didn't know you shipped on a slaver did you, boys?" asked Bernard.

"He's going to sink us if he don't stop drivin' this boat. Why she's older than he is, and we all seen them rotten places along her keel. Another thing—he ain't reefed her sail. Cap'n Bart would be crazy if he knew the old man was carrying every lick of rag in this breeze. Stay clear o' that mast, I tell you. She'll be coming down right soon."

"Heave."

"Ho."

The decks of *Ruby Ford* flexed as the dredges bit into the thick bed of spat oysters. Sometimes the dredges would load within seconds, and the weight of the loaded scrapes would make the skipjack shudder and almost stop. It was always this precise moment, when the bow of the boat seemed to trip on something and threaten to pitch down into the seas, that the old captain signaled his crew to haul their dredges. Each time the dredges dug into the bottom and the vessel began to shudder the crew wondered whether the captain would be quick enough to haul the dredges before the strain of the mast or rigging was too much. They thought about the cracks in the mast and the rot along the keel.

"Heave."

"Ho."

Hundreds of pounds of spat crashed aboard *Ruby Ford* each minute. The men took off their heavy clothes, rolled up their shirt sleeves, and started to sweat as they shoveled the spat into huge piles that began to cover the deck of the skipjack from bowsprit to wheel. The speed of the operation and the heat of the day caused the crew to ignore the wondering stares of other crews and the mutterings of their queer captain. The rhythm of the labor made them chatter thoughtlessly.

"Thought the old man's liver'd given out on him."

"That's what I'd heard, too. Bart told me they took the old man up to Easton for a week."

"Hospital?"

"To dry him out. Had the DT's. Found the captain locked in the bathroom one day—screamin' his heart out."

"God, he's a devil."

"Doctors sent him home. Said he was a goner; liver was played out."

"Now he's pirated this here drudgeboat!"

"Shows just what the doctors know, don't it?"

"Ain't one of them can figure that old man."

"Ain't me either."

"He's just balls. That's the end on it. More juice than them prize bulls they got up the road."

"Juice, you say. 'Bay Rum' I call it. Look there."

The crew eyed their master. He leaned on the wheel even more noticeably than he had when they had first seen him. His face thrust forward as if straining to call to his crew. At regular intervals he freed an arm from the wheel and reached inside his coveralls. He tossed an open pint of liquor to his lips. The shirtsleeves wiped the mouth clean.

"Heave, you monkeys," came the captain's call. "Break your backs to it or be damned."

"He's warmin' up now, ain't he?" said Bernard.

"Hot as a firecracker."

"Break his own back," called the mate before he had checked the shout. Then in a lower tone, "I ain't sweat so much in ten years."

The old man's eyes flashed at the mate, "I'll clear the world of you, donkey." With sudden speed and grace the captain rushed forward over the piles of oysters. As he moved over the piles, his hands clawed up spat, which he showered on the mate. Bobby covered his head with his arms

"Shove 'em overboard. Get the blasted things out of my sight. Spat oysters—fool's gold . . ."

and tried to drop behind the winding machine out of the captain's view. But the old man scrambled toward the work deck with such haste that the pock, pock, pock of the spat against the mate's oilskins sent Bobby retreating behind the oysters piled in the bow of the boat.

"One more word, jackass, and I'll drive you off the bow." The captain spun around to face the rest of the crew: "Damned if I won't. Who's goin' to make it different? Heave them drudges and mind your friend's tongue. We're not loaded yet. I want 1,000 bushels. Hear?" The captain moved back to the wheel.

The crew returned to the rhythm of haul, heave, shovel, shovel, shovel . . . The men wondered silently how the old man planned to make their skipjack carry 1,000 bushels: she was built to hold 750.

Morning passed in the swinging of shovels and the haze of sweat-soaked eyes. After an hour *Ruby Ford* began to move more sluggishly. Water came closer to her decks. Oysters covered her entire length five or six feet deep. She looked like a sailing rock pile.

A boat from the Department of Natural Resources came alongside the skipjack, "Cap'n, sir, looks like you got more'n she can carry already."

"Mind your own business," called the old man. "When I want you to tally up, I'll holler."

"I got a slip here for you; says you got 750 bushels," called the skipper of the state boat.

"Go away!" yelled the captain.

"I ain't goin' to let you sink those boys, Cap. May as well haul your drudges 'cause I am payin' for 750. That's it."

"Screw."

"That's all," said the official. "Take the ticket, Bobby." The mate reached out and took the receipt from the man on the powerboat steaming to windward of the skipjack.

"Goddamned government bastards," screamed the old captain. He spun *Ruby Ford's* wheel. The skipjack crashed against the powerboat as that vessel veered to pull away.

"Just go plant that spat, Cap'n. Got no time for your foolishness."

The old man made a deep rasping sound as he cleared his throat and spat at the stern of the powerboat. He froze for seconds in the act of projecting the spit.

The crew watched their captain. At last he seemed to recover from a daydream. "Sheet out them sails," he said. "We got some plantin' to do."

It was a blue steel day and an hour's sail to the planting bar. The crew lay back on the spat and rested. Small seabirds, called shearwaters, hovered over *Ruby Ford*. The captain steered in silence and drank.

The crew's sleep was disturbed by the slurred words of the old man: "Shove 'em overboard. Get the blasted things out of my sight. Spat oysters—fool's gold. Wasted my life. Shove 'em quick. Got to go home."

"Drunk as a coot," muttered Bernard. "Let's get it over with 'fore he gets any worse."

They were on the planting bar. The six crewmen swung their shovels and the spat settled into the Bay. The captain left the *Ruby Ford* to steer herself. He slouched over the rail and gazed at the swirling, sinking spat. He seemed to watch his shadow gliding among those rings. By degrees the boat emptied and the scowl dropped from the old man's face.

"Hey, boy, come aft here!" The captain pointed to Bobby. "You, boy, come!"

Bobby threw a questioning look at Bernard.

"Don't ask me: can't explain 'bout that old man."

Bernard slapped Bobby on the butt, "Don't say nothin' but 'yes sir.' "

"Come boy." The man's speech was thick; he waved his arms wildly in the air.

Bobby crawled over the heaped spat to the stern.

"Take the wheel. Sail her. Don't care where. Just unload her quick and get me home."

Bobby wasn't at all sure where the boundaries of the planting bar were, so he brought the *Ruby Ford* about and began resailing the path along which they had just planted spat. It was a route he could follow until the decks were clear.

"Steady, boy, bottom's goin' to fall out o' this breeze directly. It's comin' to a mild wind and a deep blue sky. Sixty years ago. Day like this I sailed my daddy's drudgeboat. Caught my first arsters, planted my first spat. Sixty years of chill and hazard and storms. Years of loneliness at the

"Lord, what is that thing
that kept crowding me away from the hay fields?
Always the catch . . ."

wheel. Called a bastard and demon. Why? Why forsake the meadowlands and a woman—left to grow old and die before her time while I was not noticin'?"

The old man sipped steadily from his pint of rum. Bobby tacked *Ruby Ford*. The crew rushed to unload the boat. The breeze was dying.

"Sick with the thought of water, boy. Sick with the torment of the sail and the catch. Feel bent and breathless with a million bushels of arsters on my back. Lord, what is that thing that kept crowding me away from the hay fields? Always the catch. The catch is the thing. Where's the peace in it? A mild breeze and a blue sky? That's the pay and that's the bait! Is it enough for you? Is it enough for any man?"

The old man took a gulp of rum and flung the bottle into the waves. "Sick and drunk," he muttered. "Take me home." The captain disappeared into the cabin below.

When the last spat sunk in the Bay, the crew rigged the push boat and furled the sails. The old man curled like a dog on the cabin floor and dozed. No one tried to explain the events of the day. Dredging was over until the fall.

(From *Watermen* by Randall S. Peffer by permission of The Johns Hopkins University Press, Baltimore, MD 21218. Copyright ©1979.)

GROSSE POINTE TO APURASHOKORU AND BACK

(BUT NOT QUITE BACK)

BY MIMI DYER

Even for South Seas connoisseurs, this was an extraordinary anchorage. In the snug embrace of green-tufted islands, jagged with limestone stalagmites and spiky with sword palms—accessible only through a single, all-but-invisible entrance—*Rabbit* lay easily to her anchor, marking time with diurnal swings. These anchorages were a cherished respite from the heads-up exhilaration of brief Trade-wind passages—in this case our last such passage in the Pacific. □ Apurashokoru, this edenic cove with the impossible name, lay in the 70-mile-long lagoon of Palau, in the Western Carolines. Here once-in-a-lifetime mornings and afternoons spun out with snorkeling through aquamarine water over fine white coral sand. Huge iridescent-lipped tridacna clams seemed to smile while feeding. A sailfin surgeonfish hoisted its dorsal fin like a fully battened sail. Up in the air-breathing world, noddies and frigates circled lazily—from habit; they found easy grazing on still sea meadows teeming with life. Doves, unseen, mourned in the hot greenery all around us.

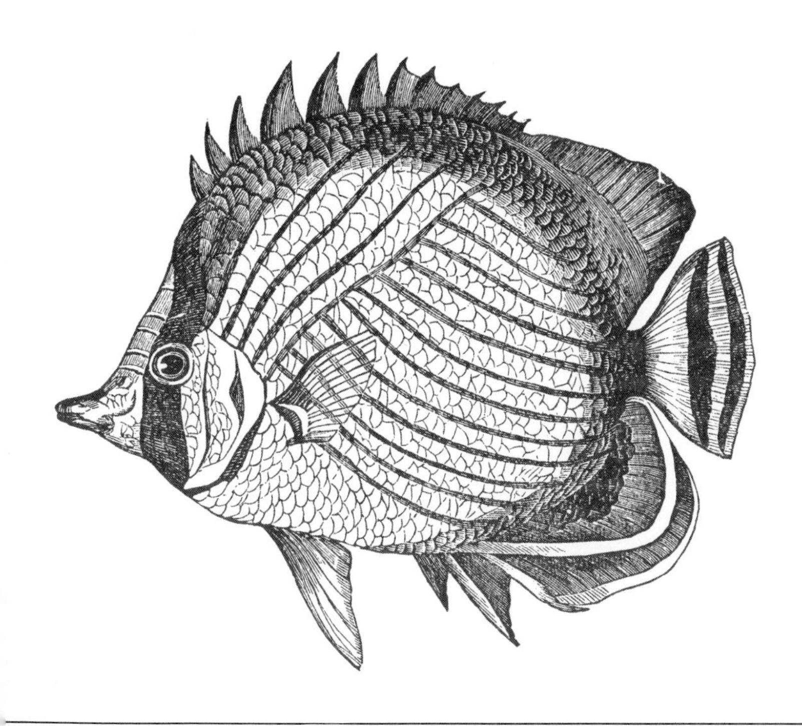

We are all boat people, huddled masses yearning to breathe free, longing to flee the warty known for the shimmering unknown. Reaching for the ring, staking our pile on the high of beating the house . . .

Darkness brought a light-show of phosphorescent wrigglers corkscrewing upstream beside the boat, and we leaned over the rail in fascination at their bright antics. This was the most enchanting spot we had seen in five years and 22,000 miles.

A Christmas gift from friends at home awaited the right circumstance, and this was it. Restless creatures, we demand texture, counterpoint in our lives—one reason we found ourselves in a Micronesian paradise after seven years in challenging careers in Detroit.

So, having assembled a uniquely Yankee feed on the foredeck—hot dogs, peanuts, popcorn, beer—we violated the Palauan night with oompah tape recordings of the University of Michigan marching band and a nasal play-by-play of the previous fall's UM-Ohio State football game. Not that we were homesick, or that this spot, this evening and this trip were not enough. They were, in fact—even after all those miles and years and heady experiences—just a little unbelievable. Hearing the twang of the hometown sports announcer was like pinching ourselves. Hey, we are here! Midwestern folks in wonderland.

It had begun mundanely. Coming down off the high of *Dynamite*'s successful Canada's Cup campaign, we were ripe for something. Subcutaneous seven-year itch, species suburbanus. Then the boat Dan had fallen in love with—a Black Watch 37—became available. We bought her. A week later he pointed out, with provocative logic, that "we really can't afford to keep a boat we have no time to use."

And that is how two people came to scratch the itch. Eight months later we set off on a dream cruise we gave ourselves little time to dream about—what with selling the house, stashing the furniture, training job replacements, taking celestial and scuba courses, readying the boat and ordering hundreds of charts, a windvane, radios and other distance-cruising gear.

Dreams, we knew, had a way of staying just over the horizon. And eventually they had a way of becoming never. Wait until those loose ends are tidied up? Not really. Loose ends stay loose until the Green Ripper tidies them permanently. There is no perfect time. You pays your money. The itch is a constant, a given, a universal that goads the restless, questing, greedy spirit of man. Yin seeks yang. Positive seeks negative. Male seeks female. Urbanites seek the country. Farmhands seek city lights. We sought South Sea Islands, where we found village youth shipping aboard interisland trading boats to seek something in Papeete, Suva, New Zealand...

We are all boat people, huddled masses yearning to breathe free, longing to flee the warty known for the shimmering unknown. Reaching for the ring, staking our pile on the high of beating the house, pushing the edge of the envelope. Yet how much dream there is in our doing, how much doing in our dream, determines how we make out. Dreams perpetuate themselves, but they do not fulfill themselves. People fulfill dreams—by choosing among options and then making those most-wanted things happen. Two roads diverge in a wood; you cannot take the one less-traveled and the one more-traveled, too.

The dream, for us—little lingered over, dwelt on only subliminally while our conscious minds framed the plan—was an extended cruise that, for all we knew, would be just like a short cruise except longer, to places unreachable on the short umbilical of workaday lives. There would be—this much we knew—effortless sailing in the Trades, jewellike anchorages, barefoot beachcombing along stretches of sole-searing sand, time to read, time to think, time to slow down and branch out from the closed-course race our lives had become . . .

The plan, meanwhile, was structured by the people we then were. A tight schedule, typed by Dan's secretary, called in the short run for a whistle-stop out the St. Lawrence, down the East Coast, through the Caribbean and the Panama Canal. A year later, when that schedule surfaced among boat papers, we could appraise its true worth: "Gone only a year," we wrote derisively in the log, "and already six months and half an ocean behind!"

In the long run, our plan was to gunkhole across the Pacific for a couple or three years, eventually to Japan, possibly shipping the boat home. A good, workable, sufficiently but not excessively ambitious plan, it had two salient features—flexibility and Japan—which were to make it a cruise that dwarfed the dream and surpassed the plan.

Leaving—pulling out of the home slip and starting off—was one of those weird occasions when you are totally wrapped in the moment. Its ordinary details (coiling lines) and its never-before-never-again bridgeburners (calling the office on UHF to pick up the company car) were there for real, yet at the same time removed, a look at your small self from a perspective. Oddly—for all that lay unknown—that we would circumnavigate, that it would take six years—one thing I did know. On the morning of day one, I knew that Wolfe was probably right; you can't go home again. That was okay, but the poignancy of knowing it complicated a skein of emotions I shied from untangling. Still, it was a giddy moment. We were doing it—busting out, snipping the cord, getting this outlandish show on the road: Dyers—1, Puritan ethic—zip.

As *Rabbit* was borne downriver on a strong current, we congratulated ourselves on this first step in that proverbial Oriental journey. Sure there were big questions that time alone could answer. How would we and the boat take to it? What if . . . What if something major broke in a remote part of the world? What if one of us had a serious accident at sea? What if we missed a landfall? What if one of us fell overboard? What if we ran into

Gradually, imperceptibly, island by island, as we sailed beyond the pull of time and deeper into the cruising life, that island temperament became our temperament, that beat our beat.

a tropical storm? What if whatever... On departure day, I was morbidly obsessed by one mundane fear: what if we ran aground in the Detroit River? Beyond that, I felt I could cope with anything.

At some point during the second week, sailing out the St. Lawrence, we realized that a racing sailor does not a cruising sailor make. Changing sails and trim with each caprice of the wind, we were going to flame out before ever reaching salt water. So one fluky afternoon, Dan hollered, "This is a *cruise,* dammit!"—then made a policy decision to go undercanvassed when in doubt, engaged the autopilot and plunged into Herman Wouk's *The Winds of War.*

The companion bit of wisdom came shortly, as we sailed around the Gaspé Peninsula in company with a French-Canadian doctor and crew. They were on a two-week shakedown of their new, home-built sloop, and they set a punishing pace, similar to ours during short cruises in Maine, the Bahamas and the Great Lakes—new anchorages every day, even lunch stops, notches in the pistol grip. An extended cruise makes more and different demands on crew and boat over the long haul. Once in the groove, we settled into an average of one offshore day in ten. Dan, who found it easier to shed the work ethic than the racing drive, was astonished to find that such a pace was typical among bluewater cruising folk.

To a working person, time is a primal reality. There is never enough of it, and it can become a great enemy. Beginning with a rude predawn alarm buzz, the warning gun of the rat race, the workday is measured in minutes and seconds. I have learned to tolerate a three-minute egg because a four-and-a-half minute egg takes too long. In cruising, we found that time spun out with marginal relevance, as if we had sailed outside its field of effect. Precise time mattered for taking noon sights; otherwise we paid no heed to the big hand or the sweep hand, only to the little hand (tides) and the calendar (full-moon landfalls, storm seasons). Satisfying though it was to put time in its place, it occasionally took us by surprise. In Venezuela, for instance, we somehow lost a month. Having planned to start for the San Blas in early October, Dan realized one late-September day that "There isn't anything between September and October!" The following year, in the Marquesas, having island-hopped, varnished and generally lolly-gagged after the month-long passage from Panama, we found we had no idea of the date. We panicked briefly: how were we to navigate to the Tuamotus without knowing the date? Then we vowed to cross off each day on a calendar when at anchor; then, three years and an ocean later, despite this system, we found a month at Bali.

If our perceptions of time were changing, so too were our rabbis. Dan's heroes had been industrial achievers—Boss Kettering, Bill Lear, Alfred Sloan. My immediate-past role model had been Helen Gurley Brown, editor, and the one before that had been Helen Gurley, all-together single girl. Now we looked to the Smeetons, the Hiscocks, Joshua Slocum, David Lewis, even Moitessier—off the wall, we concluded on meeting him, but rebounding in the right direction.

The day our country disappeared below the horizon was perhaps the true beginning, and like any rite of passage it was accompanied by endings. My farewell ice cream, three flavors stacked precariously on a sugar cone, had a sacramental solemnity about it. When the alabaster rooftops of Palm Beach condos drowned in the Gulf Stream swell, I wept for fear of the unknown. This would become, to a comedic point, the pattern of our leave-takings—tears from me and reassurances from Dan. We made a perfect Janus—Dan looking ahead, and I looking back.

With time now on our side, the alarm clock and schedule discarded like a shucked skin, we were ready for our first taste of the islands—the Bahamas and the Caribbean. In the springtime of our cruise, during a year of sailing from the Virgins down through the Leewards and Windwards to Grenada, and from Venezuela to Curaçao and Aruba, then to the San Blas and finally the Panama Canal, we first took the true measure of the island temperament, first heard the sound of that different (here, a steel-band) drummer. Gradually, imperceptibly, island by island, as we sailed beyond the pull of time and deeper into the cruising life, that island temperament became our temperament, that beat our beat.

Letters from home became less frequent, with uncertain mail stops, and we wrote home less often as new realities took our attention. It was a metamorphosis—outgrowing of old skin, acute sensitivity to new surroundings, acclimatization, more growth . . . what wonder we have had difficulty since fitting back into the old skin? Mail spanned the distance, yet emphasized it, confirming the trip and our incredible luck in doing it. Old friends wrote of a life which now seemed as remote as our Caribbean boat chores had when anticipated from that one. They were part of a once and future incarnation, but very far from the realities of the moment.

New friends were members of a special club. Occasionally we spoke, over rum punches in one another's cockpits, of the traces we had kicked over, the obstacles hurdled, the priorities reordered: family, business, money, home, our place on the socioeconomic escalator. Each of us had paid a price to crowbar himself out from between the middle-class rock and the bourgeois hard spot. We had earned these endless summers of downwind sailing, this world-girdling smorgasbord of islands, this peerless company of peers. We had paid our dues. We were made of the same stuff. Almost always we liked one another on sight. Conversations were easy and lively. They began from a shared base, yet always, always we learned from one another, because we were all learning, one reason we were there. I can say that I learned more in six years of circumnavigating than in any others except the first six.

The Caribbean was our proving ground, a school of gentle knocks

It is instead solitary freedom, and there has never been anything like it before or since. For days and nights there is only us, the boat and the sea forever around us.

whose lessons, learned at little cost, would serve us well winding through the Pacific, across the Indian—the only ocean we sailed that didn't touch our shores—and finally again on the Atlantic. They were mostly basic lessons, yet they needed to be learned nevertheless in the field, fancy talk for having to burn your hand on the hot stove. No partying before passages. New skills—celestial—take practice. Look before you leap (Dan having vaulted out of the dinghy into a stand of fire coral, I into a shallow bed of sea urchins). Listen to weather forecasts twice daily, even at anchor. Don't read off-watch if you can sleep. It amounted to arranging the breaks on your side, hugging the windward edge of a pass, hoarding your rainy-day chips, because you never knew. "There's justice out there," was my oft-expressed suspicion, "but very little mercy." Boss Kettering, I like to think, would have agreed.

No crystal ball was needed to foresee which crews were going to have what kind of a time. And although those who persisted in *ad-hoc*ing it—stamping out brush fires—had some splendid adventures, too, they missed a whole dimension, the high of feeling you're doing it well, *maxing* it. There lay the heart of the matter for us—the soaring, freewheeling, anything-possible, rebel-yelling sense that this life experience is going at hull speed, and going well.

For us, a sound operating policy lay behind the apparently sanguine assumption of Dyer's Law, which is: "Whatever can go wrong probably won't." This had always seemed a posture of mental bravado, but no. The idea was: know the odds, improve them every chance you get, and hope the Great Croupier comes through.

And he came through at Panama, in a squeaker we accepted as a talisman. Approaching the small, entry-port island of Porvenir, in the San Blas, we picked our way through an encircling maze of coral heads. Finally there was a clear shot, close inshore, to the anchorage. All at once a single-engine airplane dropped out of the late-day sun, heading for the runway abeam of us on a course that would shorten our rig. We braced. The pilot yanked her up and around, her sluggish response telling us all we needed to know. Whew!

The Canal transit, after a year in the Caribbean, was the real rite of passage. We were ready—for the big ocean, the long crossings, the main course, the sea-girt world in macrocosm as we planned and navigated, in microcosm as we sailed and beachcombed and dove. We knew then what to expect of one another and the boat, and what to demand of ourselves.

There was a lot of water out there—4000 miles across to the Marquesas, four down to the great squid. Despite every reasonable expectation of an easy passage, I was apprehensive. A month or more at sea was simply overwhelming in the aggregate, much as I enjoyed its likely components. But there must be something to it; South African friends had remarked on their reluctance to step ashore in the Caribbean after an Atlantic crossing. Were they *kidding?*

They were not. By the time *Rabbit*'s chain rattled out at Fatu Hiva, her crew were confirmed passage freaks. *Trade-wind* passage freaks. It had been just the sort of passage a bluewater sailor's addiction is made of. Any voyage that begins with a good weather forecast and with crew and yacht in top form is off to an auspicious start, but a dolphin sendoff is the ultimate thumbs-up. From the mouth of our anchorage, more than a dozen dolphins exuberantly matched *Rabbit*'s pace, flanking her with a choreography of leaps, rolls and interweaving ensemble numbers that lasted at least two hours. Moitessier wrote that dolphins had saved him and *Joshua* once, south of New Zealand, preventing him by right-hand turns in repeated—and he thought, thoughtful—formation from fetching up on Stewart Island, "hidden in the stratus." To us they merely said "Godspeed!" But if you believe in dolphins, and I do, it was a benediction from Neptunus Rex.

What is it about passagemaking that bluewater sailors cherish? Isn't it boring? Two people on a 37′ boat with nothing to see or do and no one to talk to for four weeks? It sounds like Dr. Johnson's notion of being in a ship. It is instead solitary freedom, and there has never been anything like it before or since. For days and nights there is only us, the boat and the sea forever around us. In this self-contained universe the feeling of control (honed by awareness that all our tomorrows may be canceled at any moment) is nearly total; the peace is palpable; the unity of purpose and direction is unprecedented—yacht, crew, Trade wind and current all flowing as one. We are someplace else. The exquisite rightness of things seems to nourish the air we breathe and our coursing blood and the teeming sea. The passage is a many-splendored singleness remarkable for its freedom from fragmentation—the quintessence of quality time. It is brimful of necessities and pleasures and, as you might expect of an earthly heaven, the necessities are a pleasure, and the pleasures become necessary. Navigating, keeping an eye on course and trim, cooking, exercising, acquiescing to randy rhythms of the romping yacht, dropping into a Mickey-Finn sleep, observing the bright blue world. There are—it's a throwaway line—worse ways to pass the time.

Landfall came indeed as an intrusion, but a miraculous one—Fatu Hiva dead ahead after only 29 days, found by ancient science perfected by quartz watch. Polynesia and the islands beyond. At last. What we came for. The islands were as sensuous and other-worldly as our expectations, and their easy people became our friends. But what transported us was the special world framed by our face masks. In the Caribbean we had fallen fins over snorkel in love with the undersea world, its ballet of gaudy tropical fish, gorgonians swaying among hard corals, mollusks on their tedious march, and the silent, swift drama of predator and victim. And now, in the Pacific, our time in and under the water was rich in fun, beauty,

In the rugged Torres Islands . . . havoc wrought by some violence of nature—earthquakes, possibly—had left coral and huge clam shells uprooted, like bodies on a battlefield.

even lab lessons in nature's food chain, somber reminders of man's place in a natural order in which protein is gourmet fare. And always surprises.

Dan went night-diving for crays with the young lions of Fatu Hiva. Didn't they worry about sharks? They laughed and shook their heads. Later, at a crayfish feast in *Rabbit*'s cabin, warmed by the kerosene lantern, I found that the Marquesans had simply hugged the underwater cliffs, keeping the American yachtsman between them and any sharks.

In the Lagoon at Takaroa, in the Tuamotus, I swam above a serpentine furrow in the sand that I was confident would lead me to an auger shell, buried at the end of it. What I found instead, to my disgust, was the business end of Dan's spear, which he had been trailing as he swam along the bottom.

In the rugged Torres Islands at the northern end of the New Hebrides, havoc wrought by some violence of nature—earthquakes, possibly—had left coral and huge clam shells uprooted, like bodies on a battlefield. Deeper, the destruction was on a grander scale, canyons and amphitheaters scored by jagged fissures.

At Naviti, in Fiji's Yasawas, threading the full-keeled *Rabbit* through an unforgiving coral-rimmed pass, we dropped anchor precisely in the middle of a snug, scarcely-room-to-swing-the-cat cove. Diving to investigate what looked from the foredeck like a large coral head, we found a single-place airplane with a school of sergeant majors playing in its cockpit.

This panoply of flora and fauna was strongly affecting, an infinitely intricate system whose self-perpetuating and vivid beauty was all the more wondrous for existing in a medium that found us at the mercy of our air supply. I was a lucky intruder, and I wanted to contribute, to express the experience in some fitting way, to celebrate another reality with a paean, to compose an "America the Beautiful" for its undulating fans and darting chromis and hungrily clamoring polyps, for its coral palaces and humping turtles and sycophant crabs and sashaying fire wrasses, for a reality that survives very nicely without us. I wanted to bring all the children from our air-breathing world—for just a day, an hour—to the world down there, so they would have a glimmer of what there is to see and feel and know and be.

As we sailed downwind in the reliable Trades, there was plenty of good company among like-minded cruising folk, many of whom, by now, were friends, as our paths crossed along the milk run. It was fat-cat cruising; it was summertime, and the livin' was easy. We went that way for all the time-honored, unassailable reasons, when that way lay the places we wanted to see. Otherwise we peeled unhesitatingly off the beaten track, and that way lay untold riches.

Suva is to the Pacific what Chicago is to the United States. The year we were there (1976) 180 foreign yachts passed through, most of them simply notching Fiji into the old pistol grip and moving on to Pago Pago, Vila, Auckland. Some ventured, as we did, on a beam reach to Fiji's Yasawa group. But only we tireless, hard-core, manic, backwoods cruising types made it to the Lau group, paying for it—after the obligatory check-in at Suva—with a nasty upwind sail, two overnighters in a reefy area. Worth every penny in fun and friendships. Like that of Lewis, a bright and funny Fijian 12-year-old who attached himself to Dan. One morning Lewis, invited to sail aboard *Rabbit* to the next village, showed up in some not-quite-Breton reds. "Wore my red pants," he said, reaching for the tiller, "because red pants is Skip."

Nasty sails—and they were few—were almost invariably followed by great ones. The ride back to Suva from the Laus was such a one—a broad-reaching joyride in 25 knots, with whitecaps effervescing on an indigo sea mirrored by cumulus scudding across a cerulean sky. *Rabbit* reveled in the conditions in her graceful way, a bit headstrong and yet forgiving—surfing down the face of a wave, starting to round up, thinking better of it, falling off into the groove again. She loves being slightly overcanvased in an easy sea, smoking along on the fine edge of control, just shy of wiping out. Right where she and we and you get our biggest kicks. It was rambunctious sailing, and we took turns steering, partly because the windvane didn't quite have what it took, but mainly for the sheer hell of it. We were going so fast it made you want to have hands on the tiller in case that moment came when she actually lifted off, sailed *right up out of the water and flew.*

The day was so impossibly blue and the sailing so wild as to distort reality by exaggeration, like a fisheye lens, making you more in than out of the scene, the moment—a bizarre awareness that this is what you were born for, this is *it*. You are Michael in Peter Pan, soaring over the nursery, exulting at your own cleverness. Everything you are you are bringing to this moment, making the most of it and it you. And although you think you earned it, you are a speck in it, here on sufferance and almost by the way. A day like that is a whole and perfect gift.

The place was Fiji, an island nation of such compelling fascination that friends with us in the Laus were on their second circumnavigation—because they gave it too short shrift the first time around. But it could have been any of a number of places, because this place seems, as are others in those seas, a metaphor for the universe, a moment one for all time while you are all mankind experiencing everything. There are too few moments like this in most of our lives, but bluewater cruising held more of them than anything we had known before.

And backwoods cruising held the most—naturally, and for the same reason that people who think the world owes them a living make a very poor living: givin' is gettin'. So it happened that Uncle Sam, specialist in cramming rhomboidal pegs into trapezoidal holes, godfathered the best two years of our lives, by sending a young Yankee with seafaring blood in

This was Dyer-San, Japanophile and sailor, coming home to a country he loved and a legendarily inscrutable people he understood. If ever anyone maxed an experience, Dan maxed Japan.

his veins and an insatiable curiosity to Japan. Stationed there for 18 months, Dan had made enough of his time that the country gave back to him enough that he would sail halfway around the world to visit it again. Japan determined our route in the western Pacific, which holds all the places whose names come up when we play a game we might call "If you could plunk *Rabbit* down anywhere in the world for two weeks . . .?" Japan made possible Truk Lagoon before and the glorious Western Carolines and seething Moluccas afterward.

Truk. A very plain name for the most spectacular place I have seen in what started out as a plain life but took an interesting turn around the world. We went to Truk to see the garden. Price of admission was the crummiest sail, start to finish, in six years—a near-miss with a container ship the first night out, too overcast to get sights most days, squally, current setting us east toward Kapingamarangi, where we had wanted to go, weather permitting, but now wanted desperately to avoid. Finally, we made landfall too late in the eighth day to risk closing with Truk and had to lay off, sailing back and forth all the blustery night between islands we couldn't see. The next day rewarded us with a perfect sail, rollicking back up to the south pass on a close reach in 20 knots of air. Truk is unique—a 40-mile-wide lagoon in which a dozen major islands, tips of a submerged volcano, rise as high as a quarter mile from the sea.

And the garden—a profusion of marine life that includes the world's most spectacular growth of soft corals, according to a marine biologist at Guam, flourishing on the hulks of the Japanese fleet sunk there in the February and April blitzes of '44. Diving down the baroquely encrusted bow mast of the 436′ aircraft transport *Fujikawa Maru,* where unafraid tropicals darted brightly among the sponges and corals and algae, we landed gently on the deck and recognized with difficulty a bow gun, garlanded with more than 30 years of marine growth. A pair of binoculars underfoot set the mind to thinking of the human tragedy that planted this garden. Thousands of men, theirs and ours, died here, where now thousands of life forms flourish as nowhere else. As I drifted down into the murky number-two hold, my fins landed on the fuselage of a Zero. My depth gauge said 90 feet. A pufferfish eyed me triangularly, with the stolid look of one who was there before you came and will be there after you are gone. That seemed to be the one of the many messages of this death-dealt explosion of life. Truk, with its silent antiphon of dirge and hallelujah, would haunt us, and never more than in the living Japan.

Japan, the place that at bottom had made our circumnavigation happen, was an emotional homecoming for Dan, a place that made me see how true it was that, whereas some people lose themselves in travel, others find themselves. I watched—as an outsider, almost a stranger—his brimming pleasure as *Rabbit* sailed up Kagoshima Bay to the port of entry. And watched in amazement this old-shoe guy, this high-school language dropout bowing the port officials ceremoniously aboard and greeting them volubly in what seemed to be fluent Japanese. Saw that he had his *meishi,* or calling card, at the ready when they produced theirs. Who *was* this man? This was Dyer-San, Japanophile and sailor, coming home to a country he loved and a legendarily inscrutable people he understood. If ever anyone maxed an experience, Dan maxed Japan. That he had sailed his yacht halfway around the world to get there made him a prince among princes, and that he spoke their language in more ways than one made him a trusted friend. By the time we left he had almost as many friends, old and new, in Japan as at home, and for the seven months we cruised there we were almost never alone. Among new friends were the owner of a handwoven-kimono cottage industry and the chief officer of a computer-controlled 450,000-ton tanker. Another was an international investor whose proudest boast was that his forebears were "real pirates" in the Sea of Japan 400 years ago; a racing sailor with an Admiral's Cup series under his belt, this man has two ambitions, which he spoke of in a recent letter: to meet Dyer-San in New Orleans one Mardi Gras, and to field an America's Cup contender.

The Japanese are tireless questioners, and Dan's answers always seemed to go down well, particularly when delivered in Japanese. The question they asked most often—"What is the motto of your cruise?"—struck me as odd. But Dan saw that not having such a thing discomfited them, so he thought one up, based on the name of our boat, what with rabbits being beloved creatures in Japan. And one evening, at a sake party in a friend's cockpit, he delivered the brand-new motto of our then four-year-old cruise. *"Usagi wa hayai desu,"* he declared, *"ga masugu ikimasen."* Great applause greeted this motto, which translates roughly: "Rabbits are fast, but they don't like to travel in a straight line."

If the Japanese were tireless questioners, they were also good listeners. Shortly after we berthed at Nishinomiya's Kansai Yacht Club, I wandered up to the clubhouse, where laughter and applause drew me to the conference room. There sat Dan, at a long table, answering in Japanese a barrage of questions being asked in English by eight reporters, through a lady interpreter. Coffee was being served, and four Customs and Immigration men were waiting unperturbed to finish with our papers. Leaving Japan was painful, particularly for Dan, to whom it had meant so much more than I had guessed.

Ahead lay our last island group in the Pacific, and the one that would be my own choice if I could plunk *Rabbit* down anywhere in the world—the Western Carolines: Ulithi, Yap, Palau, Helen Reef. All but unvisited by cruising yachts, peopled by Micronesians whose strong tribal fabric and sense of self brought them intact through the upheaval of World War II, these atolls were an idyllic interlude of lagoon anchorages and an undersea world beyond imagining. Palau, nourished by four confluent ocean

This was an ungentle land where volcanic islands rose abruptly from a crenulated sea floor, causing currents and rips that arm-wrestled our 37-horse diesel to the table more than once.

currents, teemed with a marine life that dazzled us, as it had Cousteau. But Helen Reef in all the world is the spot I hug to my heart, the secret place I go for replenishment when the world is too much with me. Necklace of coral, blue lagoon, one tiny sandy island (half a football field), one family. Bird life so rampant, in the absence of predators, that as I walked the beach among them, nesting blue-faced boobies regarded me with the mildest curiosity, and noddies—naturally skittish—nonchalantly fed their young. Reef life was so lush that we dove at high tide, because at low it was impossible to see the coral forest for the trees. Brazen tropicals the size of my baby finger nibbled at the human fish, darted out of range, then sped back to make another mighty raid. As the stars came out one perfect evening over joyous little Helen Reef lagoon, at the end of the earth, two American city folk, along with the lord of this fiefdom and his wife and father, sat in *Rabbit*'s cockpit discussing the incredible migrations that peopled this ocean. The old man pointed out the steering star to the ancient mecca of Mapia.

Sailing through the pass—blues paling under *Rabbit*'s keel, then deepening in open water——I felt the parting almost physically. After three years of truly pacific cruising, we were leaving the big ocean, the Trades, the easy islands and their people. We faced a brief but devious crossing, designed to circumvent the one thing that struck terror into our hearts: modern-day pirates in high-speed, high-firepowered vessels (Vietnam leftovers) in the Sulu and Celebes Seas and surrounding waters, looting and killing at will. Peer Tangvald's wife, a gun in her hand, was shot down on the deck of *L'Artemis de Pytheas,* a 450′ Japanese freighter taken hostage. Outrunning or outgunning was out of the question. The odds would be about the same as when a mongoose corners a snake. You simply had to give the known territory of the pirates (shipping lanes) a wide berth and keep a low profile. We ran without lights, maintained a wary lookout, and sailed a course that was roughly two sides of a triangle. Still, during the three days it took to reach the Northern Moluccas of Indonesia, a speck on the horizon or a light at night was enough to jerk our neck hairs out of their follicles. This was one passage the completion of which met with no mixed emotions.

The Moluccas were a brooding place of unease—unsettled and unsettling. Man against nature, with nature winning. This was an ungentle land where volcanic islands rose abruptly from a crenulated sea floor, causing currents and rips that arm-wrestled our 37-horse diesel to the table more than once. Steaming, sun-seared days of glutinous calm were obliterated in tearing rain squalls, thanks to the Intertropical Convergence Zone, guarantor of schizoid weather.

What redeemed the seething Moluccas for a couple of sailors were the native boats. Here, as everywhere, the boats said a lot about the place and the people. The Moluccans, who lived by their boats, took them straight up. Anything went as long as it *went,* and there was no conscious or decorative art, only the functional art of harnessing the force to overcome the resistance. Nothing in this strangest of all strange lands was remoter from the American way of life and yet closer to our hearts than the Moluccan's engineless working sailboats, from stately schooners to slender *perahu*. And these were people, in so many ways incomprehensible, who genuinely enjoyed sailing their boats. One afternoon during a ferocious squall a sailing canoe came screaming past our anchored yacht, dead downwind and yawing wildly, the blown-out patched panels of its holey sail beating mad tattoos in the air while—crouched behind a fish trap amidships—the scrawny skipper desperately played the sheet, grinning toothlessly in a transport of joy. He was the happiest Moluccan we ever saw, and the only one we truly understood.

As so often before, the all-wise Justice laid it on thick in both pans of the scale. On the trip from the Moluccas southwest toward Bali, one final pitch-black squall was followed 24 hours later by an incomparable night—the loveliest coastal cruising we have ever known. A full white moon lit the jagged crater of Gunung Rindjani, on Lombok Island east of Bali. The shore breeze obligingly rounded the northwest corner of Lombok with us, staying an ideal 60° off our bow. Ghost ships glided across *Rabbit*'s path—topsail schooners, their sails like black paper cutouts against the immaterial moonlit gray. On my midnight watch, with the assurance of a large-scale chart and the moon (and little trusting the wind to bend around the corner with us), I hugged the shore until I could see and hear the surf. Now I could smell seaweed, fish and reef. I sang softly—"Who will buy this wonderful evening?" Dan, coming up on watch, would not buy it at such close quarters, and pulled the steering vane back down.

The slight emotional chill—a cloud passing over the sun—was a condition of which the pirate scare was only a symptom. The chill was a first inkling that this cruise, this life within our lives, was coming to its autumn, although there were Indian summers of warm days and places. Joyously knowable Bali was one. There would be others. But the trip and the cruising life were no longer endless. Though only halfway around the world, we would be home in a year, and it would be over. The best, with some solid-gold exceptions, had been.

Nothing lay between us and Africa at Bali but 5000 miles of the Indian Ocean. That was all. A few islands, to hit or miss as weather dictated, and a date three months off, circled on the ship's calendar and never far from our thoughts—the onset of the cyclone season, before which we must reach Durban. Very little good had been written or said of the Indian Ocean. A captain with his master's ticket and more sea miles under his belt than anyone we know had called it the most ornery body of water in the world. Yet it was good to us. Boisterous at times, both in and out of the Trades, maddeningly flat or squally, it gave us a lot of splendid sailing.

Then through the pink twilight haze, a shadowy land mass materialized—Africa! My thoughts reeled from wildebeest and zebra to vineyards and the Great Karroo desert . . .

This was the first time we'd had a sense of crossing an ocean (you could say we had gunkholed across the Pacific). We were back on the well-traveled road and would be the rest of the way. Riding the Indian Ocean high, the class of '78 sailed southwestward—in touch by radio, sharing emotional as well as barometric highs and lows, punctuating passages of five to 21 days with jolly island interludes.

At Cocos, snug in a turquoise lagoon, a motley international group played all the cherished cruising games—diving, beachcombing, barbecuing, yarning, swapping books for various sea conditions. Antoine, a French rock star singlehanding an ungainly steel centerboard ketch, found no takers for his Proust. "Proust," he confessed, "will suffer only a Force Three." This was our last lagoon, and the good times had a special savor.

At Reunion, last stop before Durban, hitching across to the meteorological laboratory, we scoped out the systems currently making up between there and Africa. The accommodating director seemed unused to visits from *les voyageurs*—surprising, since we stopped at "met" offices as if they were Stations of the Cross.

As we and close friends Jim and Carol Moore readied our boats for the 1530-mile passage to Durban, I handed Carol a sealed card, to be opened on her birthday in mid-passage. Inside I had written: "Let's have a birthday rendezvous—see you at 28° 40′S, 43° 10′E!" *Tabaitha* set off a day ahead of *Rabbit*, and seven sailing days later, when Dan wished Carol happy birthday on the morning radio sked, Jim's incredulous voice came back, "Where are you? The party's at 1230, when we should be passing right over Mimi's coordinates!—we're at 28° 32′S, 43° 42′E!" With those two we shared more sea miles (out of sight, usually, but in radio contact) and more anchorages than with any other cruising friends. Having met briefly at Morehead City, North Carolina, we set out across the Gulf Stream on the same morning, in the dirty wake of a stalled hurricane, and after that we had met at Antigua, Martinique, the San Blas, Panama, the Societies, Fiji, and Bali, from which point homeward we would never be more than several days or a few hundred miles apart. The closer we sailed to "home"—and the stronger my suspicion that it wasn't going to seem like home at all but like the only alien land (except for the Moluccas) we had visited in six years—the more important it became to hear a familiar voice on the radio, to glory together in a fine sailing breeze or commiserate over a filthy low. These chats made the vast, watery world seem cozy.

We almost made it to Africa without getting socked by a southwest buster. The morning of our twelfth day, within 65 miles of Durban, Jim—who had just arrived—radioed that a southwester was forecast by afternoon. These winds—the fiercer examples are called busters—blast up the east coast of South Africa at intervals of several days to a week, and what turns them into sailors' nemeses is the strong south-setting Agulhas Current along the coast. Wind against current is always messy, but at the continental shelf it can be savage. This one had our name on it. It rolled down out of a black-and-blue bruiser of a sky. The first gust pegged the anemometer, and the wind steadied out at 38-42 knots. It wasn't bad going at first under the #5, but then the notorious seas started to build, until by late afternoon they were as wretched as any we've encountered. Keeping a proper lookout was impossible. Rather than risk closing shore, we gybed over and ran off for the night. Throughout the long night, moods swung blackly between resentment and terror as a huge crest would lift us up to reveal a tanker passing close astern. The resentment was fueled by having to put distance between us and Durban, after sailing nearly 5000 miles across the Indian Ocean to get there. Shortly before dawn, the cloud cover started to break, and by noon—24 hours after it had hit—we gybed around again for Durban.

Then through the pink twilight haze, a shadowy land mass materialized—Africa! My thoughts reeled from wildebeest and zebra to vineyards and the Great Karroo desert, from rogue waves down the coast (where we must pass on our way around the capes), to arrogant English adventurers who presided over the eradication of more than one unique species, plundering South Africa's national treasure.

Durban lies at 30° South latitude. That, I reminded Dan before we set out to sail around the continent's southern tip, was where my "contract" ran out. I would sail to the ends of the earth with him, I had said back in Detroit, "but only to the *warm* ends—south of 30° North and north of 30° South." My idea of a proper cruising climate is one where you wear a T-shirt in the heat of the day and take it off at night. Detroit itself lay outside my 30-30 parameters, at 42° North, and having sailed northeast out the St. Lawrence, at the top of the Gaspé Peninsula we were at 49°, which would be our most extreme latitude. The only other times we exceeded the two 30s were in Japan and New Zealand—Yokohama and Whangarei lying near 35° North and South, respectively. So what, I wondered as we headed out from 30° South, am I doing sailing among *penguins?* T-shirts weren't even an adequate first layer. Rounding Cape Agulhas, at the continent's southern tip, we were within 300 miles of the broken red line on the pilot chart marked "extreme limit of icebergs."

Comparing Agulhas with Good Hope, 100 miles northwest, you could see why Good Hope gets all the credit, even though Agulhas is the southermost point. Good Hope is jutting and magnificent, the stuff of great book jackets and symphonic crescendos. Agulhas, green and low, looks like a mostly melted scoop of pistachio ice cream. Then too, the waters of the Indian and Atlantic meet at Good Hope, so the distinction is more than esthetic.

Cape Town provided the last of the Indian summer stops, and we reveled in our borrowed time, plunging with backs turned on tomorrow

As we sailed closer to completing the circle, an almost breathless superstition hung in the air. We waited for the something to happen, and it never did . . .

into the living history of the place, its unnatural natural beauty, the specialness felt by all the great and simple folk who call this deeply civilized, desperately riven, blessed and cursed land home. The prospect of a transAtlantic crossing, northwestward back to the Caribbean, was inviting, with an easy downhill slide virtually assured once we had tucked away the icewater-cold Benguela current and the variables.

From Cape Town to the Caribbean was 5500 miles, about six weeks' sailing—broken into two and four by a stop at St. Helena, that precipitous volcanic pile wrapped in the mists of Napoleonic history. We approached the fortressed town, and a long-ago look in the skipper's eye gave away his thoughts as he maneuvered his stalwart frigate smartly through the roadstead, ready to gybe and run from any cannon fire.

The next and last long passage was a reprise of all the best offshore times—four twinkling weeks broad-reaching through the Trades, scarcely a hint of the doldrums except for some spectacular altocumulus, with time alone to marvel at the great blue world, time together to celebrate whatever needed celebrating—a blissful day's sailing, our fourth and final Equator crossing, a birthday. Dolphins escorted *Rabbit* across the Equator in a distinctly proprietary way, grazing her gently as if to carry the returning heroine on their backs into the Northern Hemisphere. Even things that went wrong went right, being minor and remediable. One afternoon the dreadful twang of rigging giving way jolted the boat. But it was merely a bale on the boom, fatigued and yielding to the pull of the mainsheet. We were spooked by our good luck. We had worked at arranging the breaks, hoarding our chips, but we felt we must be overdue for something after six glorious years. As we sailed closer to completing the circle, an almost breathless superstition hung in the air. We waited for the something to happen, and it never did, so maybe being spooked was an anti-hubris exercise that worked.

Awaking one early morning from a dead-man sleep, I took over the watch, slipping on my harness and stepping up into a day full of promise. Everything was possible. Seeing raw times and sextant angles Dan had left until after his morning nap, I spent the morning teaching myself how to work them out (the math, more complicated than for noon sights, had stubbornly eluded me in previous attempts). By noon I had an advanced line of position, to cross with a noon latitude. I also had a splitting headache and a sense of accomplishment that knew no horizons. By the next week, under Dan's tutelage, I could record a "perfect star fix—Regulus, Canopus and Capella."

Then one day there it was—landfall, the dim outline of Barbados, easternmost of the Caribbean islands. Journey's end, the closing of the circle, lay just an overnight sail, an island away, at lovely laid-back Bequia, where we would cross our outbound track.

Early the following morning, with *Rabbit* reaching cavalierly through Bequia Channel, as if returning from a weekend cruise to Barbados, her crew were anything but cavalier. We were polishing stainless, cleaning salt from ports, untying leecloths, stashing harnesses, pulling out cockpit cushions and—symbol of symbols—chilling the champagne. Not an hour later, shampooed and sorting through a colorful heap of courtesy flags, we hardened up into Admiralty Bay, and suddenly, miraculously, the circle was closed. We had done it, crossed our outbound track, sailed around the *world*—a thing we didn't dare imagine when we started.

When the chain rumbled out and the plow found purchase, there was nothing to do but toast the world, ourselves, each other and, not least, the forgiving lady who had carried us there and back. As we cleaned our sextants, top priority even on this day, there was an unspoken but keenly felt *je ne sais quoi*. Dan identified it later in terms of the mournful Peggy Lee lyric, "Is that all there is?"—a need for some small fanfare or coda.

Blasts on a ship's horn and excited shouts of *"Rabbit, Rabbit—Welcome Home!"* brought us bounding into the cockpit, where we beheld the entire family of our dearest friends waving from their yacht, flourishing signs that had been crayoned hastily for the occasion as they sailed up the bay.

What remained—and it has taken time—was to reenter, to decompress from an extraordinary environment which, though first seeming strange, shortly became natural—the boatshoe that fit. Sailing around the world was easy. Coming home was tough. There we were with a wardrobe of cutoffs and exotic T-shirts coming back to business suits and attaché cases. The Catch-22 was a formidable one—such a trip raises expectation levels beyond the ability of your average American life to produce. No reason not to go, but having gone, having heard the music of the spheres, one shouldn't be surprised to find oneself mortgaged to the piper.

As I write this, *Rabbit* waits out a Rhode Island winter with a Christmas wreath tied to her tarp. She prefers a sparkling, aquamarine bone in her teeth . . . Our wayward thoughts need watching. Yet we have become what we have done, seen, learned. After 47,000 miles, 40-odd countries and six years, it was in a way that counts an interior journey, what Wolfe called a "geography of the heart's desire, a magic domain of fulfillment." With time, quality time—offshore, underwater, gunkholing a remote archipelago—and breaks arranged according to Dyer's Law, so that what could go wrong probably wouldn't—we found out who we were and what we could become. A heightened sense of self—enhanced and tempered by all the things seen, experienced, understood—was a useful souvenir to bring back in the mental duffel, worth any number of straw hats or seashells. Yet like any other piece of cerebral baggage it is not entirely to be trusted, triggering the thoughts it does sometimes while we drive to challenging jobs from a lovely old house near the sea— "It's a fine life, but we know there's a finer . . ."

HOBIE ALTER

ATHLETE, ENTREPRENEUR AND BEACHCOMBER

BY PAT DAY

He has been described as *laid-back,* an expression born and well-observed in the land of free firsts, California, the state where he was born and where he stuck, glued in a very essential way to the sea.

Hobart Laidlaw Alter was not a vice-president in anyone's administration. If you shouted out the name, no one would salute, dial their broker, or swoon. Hobart L. Alter is known by the name of his boat—Hobie.

If you asked, "What's a Hobie?" more than 100,000 owners would say, "That's my boat." They might also say, "It's a lollipop-colored, wind-propelled, speed machine, and I'm crazy about it."

Three kids would say, "Sure, he's my dad."

A spokesman for a major American corporation would say, "Yes, he works here."

The BMW dealer in Capistrano, California, would say, "I told him that a man in his position shouldn't be truckin' around in an old Dodge van. He wouldn't listen."

A few women would say, "No comment."

Pie-in-the-sky entrepreneurs would say, "All I want to do is find his combination."

And therein lies the rub.

Hobie Alter is a success in Morse code, and it takes more than a few dit-dit-dit, dah-dahs, to understand why. He has been described as *laid-back,* an expression born and well-observed in the land of free firsts, California, the state where he was born and where he stuck, glued in a very essential way to the sea. Hobie is more than the designer of a 16′ catamaran that ranks third in popularity and growth rate among American one-design racers. He's more than the man who produced and marketed a sailing product engineered for people who wanted on-the-water recreation minus the chores of boat maintenance. Alter put his customers on the water and into a fun, safe, altogether exhilarating experience. And they put him into big business.

"I was a nothing kid with get-by grades," Hobie Alter tells me. He is on the floor, feet propped against the wall to ease his back, crimped during a coast-to-coast flight. His words carom, slip-sliding, one into the other. "I was skinny, only 5′2″ and 120 pounds. I loved sports like football, basketball... But forget it for midgets."

Today Alter stands a very average 5′11″ and weighs 170 pounds. In cutoffs and a T-shirt, he resembles a physically fit Mr. Green Jeans. If you saw him on the beach at a Hobie regatta in the inevitable circle of admirers, you might notice a hitch in the way he stands. It's a clue to an inherent shyness among strangers; it belies his many skills, among them those of an accomplished, all-around athlete.

He was brought up in Ontario, California, 50 miles inland from the Pacific, the son of a man who was a citrus grower, a violin teacher and a California State Assemblyman; of a woman who, at 82, tells of two-day horse-and-buggy journeys to the coast. Alter describes his parents as solid, middle-class people, and very conservative. "My mother and father always gave us what we needed as long as we would put it to some use." Young Hobie had a bike and, "you know, the normal stuff." He enjoyed building things. "Kids don't make things any more. Not from scratch, the way I did. Today, they buy a *kit.*" There is no nostalgia in Alter's words; his tone says *it's the way it is.*

"My parents thought I could do no wrong," he says, and pauses. "As long as I did something constructive, they helped me out, gave me encouragement and a few dollars." His father financed the construction of a darkroom; photography was, and still is, Alter's hobby. One gift—skis—he snapped on seven days a week after school, to run the slopes at nearby Mount Baldy. Skiing was a sport where size didn't matter. He got good. As a Class A competitive skier in the early 'fifties, he was invited to the U.S. Olympic tryout camp. He didn't go.

"For me, the excitement in a sport is working at it hard; when you hit that big bulge in the learning curve... At the top, the pressure to stay there takes the fun out of it." At 46, the creator of the boat and the sport continues to compete in Hobie World and National Championships, ranking in the top ten in a field of 72 competitors whose age averages about 22.

The Alter family lived in a pleasant house and had a sensible car. They also owned a summer place at Laguna Beach, in those days a beach bum's heaven. During the summer, the family migrated to the beach cottage. Alter started surfing—mostly body surfing—right away, and finally acquired a paddleboard. "The guys at school didn't know what a surfboard was back then," he recalls. "But I did, and that was enough." This was another sport where size didn't count. He practiced and eventually placed third in the Makaha International Championship, which was the major surfing contest at the time. He was also the Pacific Coast Tandem Champion.

He looked ahead and saw the appeal that a beachable, high-speed, low-maintenance boat might have to active water lovers with a few bucks to spend for an on-the-water toy.

Before Hobie Alter began building and competing aboard world-class little catamarans, he began building and competing aboard world-class surfboards. The time was the 'fifties, as the haircuts indicate, and the boards were among the best in the world. He started in 1954 with balsa boards shaped in a beach-house garage, then pioneered with foam-core fiberglass boards and set up a factory. He was then, as he is now, not only a builder and innovator but a tough competitor aboard his own products.

At 16, Hobie, the puny kid, copied a 220-pound friend's surfboard. He started building his board in the beach-house garage, finished it sitting shirtless in the sand, knocking off a few bumps he didn't like on his own model. It was a good board. It was fast. "One day a guy came by with cash in his hand and wanted to buy my board. He paid me more than it cost to build," Alter tells me with a smile. "I thought that was fine."

It was the beginning of a California garage industry that would grow into a manufacturing shop which Alter designed and built with $12,000 his grandfather had willed him. The year was 1954 and his first business doubled as a senior project for a junior college course in retailing. His friends told him he'd never make a living selling boards; there aren't enough people into surfing, they said. He went ahead with the project. He took a bride. He built balsa-wood boards and watched the orders pile up.

In 1957 Alter saw something new: a scrap of polyurethane foam. He thought of a way to make a better surfboard. Lighter, easier to manufacture. He was the innovator, the craftsman of the surfboard business, on top of the ninth wave. If you didn't have a Hobie or a Velzey board you weren't a serious surfer. Alter increased his production from 1700 balsa boards in his first three years of business to 1500 foam boards per year. "At the time a lot of other guys got into the surfing scene," he recalls. "I was already looking at a new idea."

Alter had a 9-to-5 job once. For three weeks he picked up the grounds at an arts festival, an experience that persuaded him to go it alone. He admits that many people aren't like he is, aren't cut from entrepreneurial cloth. "They have trouble visualizing. They see only the way it is."

He looked ahead and saw the appeal that a beachable, high-speed, low-maintenance boat might have to active water lovers with a few bucks to spend for an on-the-water toy. It would be a hybrid; something between a surfboard and a sailboat. Enter the Hobie Cat, the original 14-footer officially clocked at 23.2 miles per hour. Producing the first boat took Alter 13 months of 20-hour days and gave him an ulcer at 25. "I'm really not the worry type," he explains, "but I wrecked myself—no regular meals or sleep."

It is October, 1980, and Hobie Alter's daughter, now 26, has successfully defended her 1979 title to win the Women's National Hobie Championship at St. Petersburg Beach, Florida. "I don't remember seeing Dad too much when I was little," says Paula. "He worked all the time, every night. We didn't become really close friends until maybe three years ago, when I started racing Hobies and moved back to Southern California." Paula Alter is as wholesome as whole-wheat toast and apple yogurt, pretty, with an athletic body and a mind of her own. She spoke about earlier years with her father.

"We had homing pigeons. We'd drive the birds out into the desert in the car, set them loose, and race them back to the house." Hobie Alter and family started riding motorcycles. Every weekend they packed up the car and took off into the California desert with a tent. By now there were three children—Paula, Hobie Jr., Jeffrey—and wife Sharon. The young Alters camped in the desert, five people in a cast of 2000 competing in weekend dirt-bike races. "We all went our separate ways to race during the day," says Paula. "But we all got together with friends in the evening." Part of the sport was the camaraderie. Part was the competition. Alter filed it away in his memory bank as good, healthy western-American fun. So did his kids. "Then it was skateboards," Paula laughs. She was in the 6th grade. "We all competed on skateboards for a while."

He never dreamed of hotels overflowing, sponsor participation, package tours on jets filled with competitors and friends headed for a Hobie World Championship in places like South Africa or St. Croix.

Today more than 20,000 of Alter's innovative little first boats, the Hobie 14s, are owned by U.S. sailors. The likeness of the little machine's asymmetrical hulls and full-battened sail to Polynesian catamarans has been noted, but Alter denies any research into those ancient vessels. He knew what he wanted to achieve, studied the best boats of the type available on the market in 1967, then purchased a Pacific Cat and set about learning how to sail. "There were things I didn't like about the P-Cat," he says. "Fortunately. Because unless you really think you can make something better, why bother to make it at all?"

After 13 months of making and remaking, testing and retesting, Alter had a boat. He named it *April*. It was April of 1968. Sandy Banks, now director of the Hobie Class Association, recalled their first four-boat regattas. One boat was payment to a filmmaker for producing a promotional short on the project, one was for further testing, one was Hobie's boat and Sandy had the fourth. They called the race *A 4th of July Event*. "We bought a trophy and packed a lunch," Banks remembers, smiling and shaking his head. "When the day dawned, there was absolutely no wind." The men raced later. "We had a ball," says Banks.

Alter and partners began a stomp across the country. They were a dog-and-pony show afloat. They lined up boat dealers and organized regattas. For more than two-thirds of Hobie owners, the catamaran is their first boat, and regattas provide the fuel that fires a very big enthusiasm.

Alter was drawing on memories of days spent at surfing and motorcycle meets, the merging of action-prone people with something in common. His theory since then has been that the fun is getting together. But he miscalculated one factor—the enormity of the regatta scheme's success. He never dreamed of hotels overflowing, sponsor participation, package tours on jets filled with competitors and friends headed for a Hobie World Championship in places like South Africa or St. Croix.

"No way was this a marketing approach we backed into," says Alter. "We identified our market and knew that many of our potential customers lived far from yacht and sailing clubs. We knew if they raced a Hobie they'd enjoy the boat. We had to establish our own class, organize our own events. What was good for our customer was good for us. Still is."

But some Hobie sailors have gone beyond what's good for them, in Alter's opinion. They have exceeded prudent limitations of good seamanship by pushing themselves and their boats too far into long-distance offshore races and cruises. "I don't believe anyone should sail a small boat that does not carry lifesaving equipment farther offshore than he can swim to land," he states firmly.

Despite his father's convictions, son Hobie Alter Jr., at 24 a hotshot sailor in his own right, participated in a 1000-mile race from Ft. Lauderdale to Virginia Beach on a Hobie 16. The invitational event was the fifth-annual Worrell 1000, a race for which creator Mike Worrell provides well-organized land support systems, weather forecast advisories, and helicopter reconnaissance to safeguard those sailors he deems qualified to participate.

Nine teams started this fifth race from Ft. Lauderdale at 10 in the morning, May 28, 1980. Each catamaran carried a two-man crew and a radio. They raced north along the Atlantic Coast, stopping at checkpoints every 70-150 miles along the route to meet "pit crews" who traveled by road. At each stop they rotated crew with a third team member on the beach. "Hatteras looked mean," said Hobie Jr. "Where the 2-3 knot currents hit each other, water blasted about six feet into the air. And it was considered a mild day. It was like sailing through ten feet of washing-machine water."

The late 'fifties and early 'sixties witnessed a fervor for surfing. Two U.S. surfing magazines were launched; Bruce Brown's film "The Endless Summer" became a hit; the Beach Boys and Jan & Dean made surfing music; kids bought surfboards in places where the wait for good surf was as endless as the summer. Hobie Alter, meanwhile, was competing. Here he poses in Hawaii during a tandem-surfing contest.

Today, 300 employees work in the Oceanside, California, plant to manufacture 50 Hobies per day, 12,000 boats per year. In 1968 the company completed a total of 90 boats.

Hobie Jr.'s team covered 68 miles in three hours, 15 minutes, on that leg of the race. To do it, they averaged 20.9 miles per hour. "It was blowing 35-40, and we were going right down the beach about 10 degrees off downwind—not really reaching, but sitting on the rear crossbar and just smoking." The team finished second—in four days, 13 hours, 26 minutes.

In Europe, Holland's Round Texel Race is another example of pushing small multihulls to their limit. With 82 Hobies competing on the 65-mile race course, the class accounted for more than 25% of the registered cats. A Hobie 16 won the event, and 150 boats failed to finish due to crippled equipment.

Another brand of Hobie adventure took place in the Pacific in June, 1980. Three experienced Hobie 16 skippers departed singlehanded from San Diego's Mission Bay for a 1000-mile southbound passage. Their destination: Cabo San Lucas, Baja California. A beach crew was assembled to meet the sailors every four days. All three boats were rigged with oversized shrouds. On board were spare parts, repair supplies, tools, and food and water sufficient for nine days at sea. Only two of the three Hobies completed the passage.

"The Hobie class association does *not* approve of such races or cruises," says Sandy Banks. "The boats just weren't designed for that kind of sailing." He points out that the Baja adventure was a prime example of a trip that should never be attempted. The Hobie 16 was built for double-handling, not singlehanded sailing; the boats were sailed along a dangerously rocky and barren coastline with potential big surf conditions. "Not everyone would be lucky enough to survive," he says.

Designer/father Alter expressed strong feelings to his son about the inherent dangers of the Worrell race. Hobie Jr. wanted to do it anyway. With a corner on National Championships, he is the only Hobie sailor to have won a triple crown: in 1978 on a Hobie 14, in '79 on a Hobie 16 and in '80 on a Hobie 18. He also captured the prized Championship of Champions trophy, racing a Prindle Cat in 1979. "Attempting the Worrell 1000 without an intricate support system would be foolish and dangerous," says Hobie Sr. "But Mike (Worrell) makes it as safe as is humanly possible."

Despite class association cautions, Hobie catamarans continue to win races and make safe landfalls. And the Coast Catamaran Corporation's success stands as sporting history, an anomaly among most boat manufacturers. The outgrowth of a small-pickins' industry, the company has grown by giant steps. Today, 300 employees work in the Oceanside, California plant to manufacture 50 Hobies per day, 12,000 boats per year. In 1968 the company completed a total of 90 boats.

In 1976, only eight years after the first 14-footer was launched, Hobie Alter sold out to Coleman Industries, a Wichita manufacturer of outdoor equipment, for $3.5 million. But Alter's way of life has not appreciably changed since the cash-short days. He lives in a small glass-fronted house on Capistrano Beach. It's an older frame dwelling he bought ten years ago and has remodeled three times, in dribs and drabs. Downstairs the front room looks westward with a face of glass doors. Its size is smaller than a standard Hilton bedroom. To one side behind accordion-fold doors is a small bedroom where son Jeffrey sleeps. Behind the front room is a kitchen "a terrible, narrow place"—and a bathroom. To the rear of the house is a small bedroom where son Hobie Jr. hangs out. Hobie Sr.'s domain is above, on the second floor, an add-on consisting of a glassed bedroom and bath. "It's a great house; I love it," he says. "We've had ocean at the front windows. At times it's like a college dorm."

He tells a story about a cat burglar, a Cary Grant act-alike who ripped off a string of homes in their now-affluent neighborhood. Alter's house was full of kids. The burglar entered and snitched Paula's handbag that contained 37¢. Hobie Sr. was upstairs in his lair. Hobie Jr. reclined in his back bedroom. Jeffrey sprawled behind his folding doors. Paula, visiting for the evening, was watching television on the livingroom couch. No one heard the thief. No one knew he existed until the sheriff woke the family by phone at five the next morning, and they discovered the missing purse.

"My friends are the people I knew 25 years ago," Alter says. "They tried to convince me to buy a BMW but my Dodge van is still running pretty good, even after 90,000 miles. I can't bring myself to spend that kind of money for a car. Things where I live have changed, but I haven't. . . I go to the same bars and restaurants."

Is he a rich man? Not on the scale of best-vested portfolios. "All I want is a 25¢ return on my dollar," says Alter, no greedy man, no mere barefoot boy with cheek of tan. He has a partner to help manage his real-estate holdings ("I spent a couple of years studying that stuff"). He's on the board of directors of OP's (Ocean Pacific), a top West Coast sportswear

The antithesis of Alter's boyhood upbringing, they personify the new-breed family where parents have agreed to separate, but real estate alone divides the family unit.

manufacturer. He owns five retail stores (on the U.S. mainland and in Hawaii) selling clothing, boats, surfboards and beach gear. He wants to buy a race horse, maybe in New Zealand.

"I watch the horses at Del Mar on television in the clubhouse," he tells me with a hand-in-the-cookie-jar grin. He spends hours noodling on the scratch sheet. "If a horse has a slow start record and a position on the rail, I know it'll get boxed in." Alter figures how each race will be run, and he bets, but not too much. "I could never be a big gambler," he says.

Does he own a business suit? "Sure," he allows with a wave of his hand. "It's around the house someplace, but I haven't seen it for years." Prior to a trip East to meet with "some guys down on Wall Street," a business partner took Alter the beachcomber by the ear and brought him to a well-known men's clothing store to be outfitted. "He didn't want me to scare the bankers. And he didn't trust me to do anything as important as pick out my own suit. He was right, I guess. What do I know about business suits?"

Alter's specialty in the 'sixties was tandem surfing, an acrobatic activity in which he became Pacific Coast Champion. He also placed third in the big Makaha International contest and won scores of other surfing competitions. A remarkable thing about the Alter family is their competitive energies and successes—on surfboards, dirt bikes, skateboards and now Hobie Cats. At right, daughter Paula receives the winner's award from her father for the Women's Hobie 14 Nationals in 1980 at St. Petersburg, FL. She won it in 1979, too.

"The problem with Dad," says daughter Paula, "is that he doesn't really know what a great person he is." Paula Alter works at Coast Catamaran, now a division of Coleman, where she is the editor of The Hobie Hot Line, the bimonthly class-association magazine with 30,000 worldwide subscribers. "I came home about three years ago," she recalls. "Mom and I live together in a house on the beach at Capistrano. We're best friends." The house is two doors down from her father's, a five-minute walk.

Hobie and Sharon Alter have divorced, but their family remains intact. The two sons, Hobie Jr., 24, and Jeffrey, 19, live with their father. All five communicate with affection, share burgers, swap clothes and racing tactics, and eat Christmas dinners together. The antithesis of Alter's boyhood upbringing, they personify the new-breed family where parents have agreed to separate, but real estate alone divides the family unit.

"We all date," says Paula. "But none of us are married now. Dad tried marriage again after he and Mom divorced, but it didn't work out." The Alters are hyperactivists with goals, warm feelings for one another, and shared leisure interests. "It would be hard to top the way we live," explains Paula. "We have it so good at home together, no one wants to set up housekeeping anywhere else."

Paula had shipped inland for college at Boulder, Colorado. She missed the sea and returned to it at Cadiz, Spain, where she boarded the schooner *Westward* for a sea semester. Aboard *Westward,* she crossed the Atlantic, stopping at Madeira and the Canaries. From there it was 24 days of Tradewind sailing to Antigua in the West Indies. "I loved it," she says. Later, as crew, she delivered a boat from the West Indies to Connecticut, worked as cook aboard a Maine windjammer, sailed the Hawaiian Islands, and returned a 40′ ketch from Honolulu to Santa Cruz, California.

Paula appears a fail-safe young woman. "Oh no, I fail all the time," she protests. "If you don't ever fail, you're not trying hard enough." At Coast Catamaran, the new project she works on with her father is a 33′ monohull.

"One of my goals for the new 33 is to make a boat Paula can launch, raise the mast and rig herself," Hobie Alter says of the new project. Wanted: the largest keelboat class in the United States. That was the brief given Alter by Sheldon Coleman, Chairman of the Board of Coleman Industries, who saw the acceptance J/24s enjoyed among sport-of-the-

In the past, he had been asked twice to design bigger boats. One was a request for a catamaran to compete in the TransPac Race; one for a monohull in the 50′-60′ range. He declined both.

chase sailors. Alter works for Coleman now, but he claims negligible corporate pinch and no title. "If I had a title, I'd have to attend all the meetings. I guess you could call me a consultant."

In the past, he had been asked twice to design bigger boats. One was a request for a catamaran to compete in the TransPac Race; one for a monohull in the 50′-60′ range. He declined both. "I really don't know anything about that kind of boat," he said then. But Sheldon Coleman threw down the gauntlet in a way Alter couldn't resist, providing the multifaceted support required for a project ambitious enough to cramp the capabilities of many boat manufacturers.

Alter points out that he is far from infallible. At Coast Catamaran, he produced three boats which failed to gain wide public acceptance. "A lot of guys have the mistaken idea we can sell any good product with the Hobie name and our marketing platform. It's not quite so easy as that."

The boats that didn't make the profitability grade were smaller than the current Hobie lineup, 10′ and 12′ monocats ("sort of like baby Lasers") and a 3.5-meter version of the Hobie 14. Alter cited poor market penetration and the wrong materials (the boats were made of ABS plastic, not fiberglass) for the failure of the 10- and 12-footers. Of the 3.5 mini-cat he claims that "People who had 'em, loved 'em." The boat was an ideal size for competition by women and teens weighing between 100-135 pounds; most women carry weights to reach it. But it was too expensive; the cost for its 11.5′ came within a few dollars of the Hobie 14's price. Although production of all three boats was abandoned, Alter still sees a need for a step-up boat for young, singlehanded racers. Something just beyond Optimist prams and Sabots.

Immersed in the development of the new 33′ sloop, Hobie Alter's work habits haven't changed much over the years. His office is located in the same building where he developed and produced the Hobie Cats. But there's something new in the office now—a desk. "At Coleman there were some extra desks and office chairs hanging around. They gave me one of each, and a file cabinet." He admits his new executive suite is an improvement over sitting on a stool at a drawing board, as he once did, and stacking papers around him on the floor.

Another change is the length of his work day. He no longer toils all night, every night. Hobie now likes to go home, wants to be around the place when his sons are there in the evenings. "Could be I'm mellowing," he says. The talk at home is frequently of boats and business; Hobie Jr. is a supplier to Coast Catamaran and Jeffrey works for a custom woodshop. "With all three kids I'm more a friend than a father," says Alter. "Maybe that's wrong, but they seem to like it that way." Weekends are often spent sailing—or playing golf, Alter's latest sport. He describes himself as a rotten golfer.

> "I wouldn't go into something if I didn't think I could do it well. I'd hate to make anything that wasn't better than what's already out there. It's just too much work."

Hobie Alter Jr., meanwhile, won the Hobie 14 Nationals in 1978, the Hobie 16 Nationals in 1979, and the Hobie 18 Nationals in 1980. He also raced a Prindle Cat in 1979 to capture the Championship of Champions trophy, and competed in two Worrell 1000s, his team finishing second in 1980 and third in 1981. The Worrell 1000 is a 1000-mile ocean-racing ordeal that Hobie Sr. doesn't entirely approve. Photos on pages 41 and 43 show something of what it's like out there. The lady on page 42 shows what it's like on the beach.

But the kind of zeal associated with tent evangelists overcomes the man when he speaks of his new project—the boat that Paula can launch and rig singlehanded. His eyes narrow and dart as he snatches up a pen to sketch its retractable keel. "Initially, our idea was to hire a designer," Alter recalls. He and Sheldon Coleman worked out what they wanted in a racing/cruising sloop to compete in a market where boats are spawned as rapidly as rabbits. Their guidelines required that it be trailerable, light, aesthetically appealing, a race-winner, capable of living aboard, easily maintained and operated, and with 14-karat construction, engineering and gear. Extensive tooling would follow the design and engineering phase to permit its efficient mass production and a selling price of under $30,000.

"My file on boats ranneth over," Alter says. Of the hundreds of designs he evaluated he mentions only a handful: the Catalina 27 which he thinks is a "great, middle-of-the-road boat that gives excellent value for money," the Santa Cruz 27 and the Olson 30. These were close to what he wanted but not quite right. "I talked to a lot of competent designers and looked at a slew of boats with plenty of good features. But none precisely fit our bill." Alter decided to do it himself, from scratch.

"The monohull sailors will say, 'What does a multihull man know about a monohull?' Same as they said in '68, 'What does a surfer know about sailing?'" He says this without rancor. "I wouldn't go into something if I didn't think I could do it well. I'd hate to make anything that wasn't better than what's already out there. It's just too much work."

A prototype was launched in 1980. The boat is 33′ overall, with an 8′ beam and a retractable keel. "I don't trust daggerboards," he says. Racing under PHRF (Performance Handicap Racing Fleet) rules, the boat has already shown an impressive win record; with a course allowance of 90 seconds per mile, it has successfully licked the 174-rated J/24. On a spinnaker run from Marina del Rey to Dana Point, the new boat finished a 60-mile course in six hours.

"The way we've done the keel is unique—because it's so simple. And it's structurally sound," added Alter. To lower the keel is a ten-minute operation. It takes a mechanical winch ("we tried a hydraulic pump but too much can go wrong"), four giant lug nuts and a socket wrench. "For racing, that keel is worth its weight in gold," said Alter. With a 1640-pound lead bulb at its base, the keel accounts for 1800 of the boat's total 4000 pounds.

"This is no Spartan, stripped-out racing hull either," Alter points out. Below decks, six people can sit down for dinner, and there are two double berths, a two-burner stove, a cooler, and a head. It's a dandy overnighter, and a comfortable enough boat for a week's vacation cruise. Alter hopes to be ready for a summer 1981 introduction. "Just think," he said, "there are 100,000 Hobie owners out there who might want something else. Let's see now—if only 10 percent..."

You wouldn't call Alter a smooth kind of guy. He'd never make the cut at General Motors. A college degree doesn't hang in the den; he has neither den nor degree. You can't put the convertible top down on his Dodge van. You can't dress him up—but you *can* take him anywhere. He's a natural. You can see curiosity in his eyes about everything. You can see love in his children's faces. You can sail one of his boats and have one hell of a good time.

The closest you can come in one word to describe Hobart Laidlaw Alter is, well, successful.

On this and five following pages, lively photographs by Chris Cunningham express some of the excitement of Hobie Cat sailing and socializing. The boat is a deliberate handful, a vehicle that calls for quick reflexes and, like skiing and off-road motorcycle riding, delivers the exhilaration of ripping along on the ragged edge of control. Several of the gentlemen on pages 46 and 47 have gone over the edge, definitely part of the fun. On pages 48 and 49 are some scenes from Hobie regattas, gatherings of the faithful that are wild parties and reunions as well as sailing events.

58450
58433
58426
58419
58403
58417
58437
HOBIE 16 WORLDS
58433

400
40048

THE ELEGANT IDEM

BY JOSEPH GRIBBINS

PHOTOGRAPHS BY JIM BROWN

26

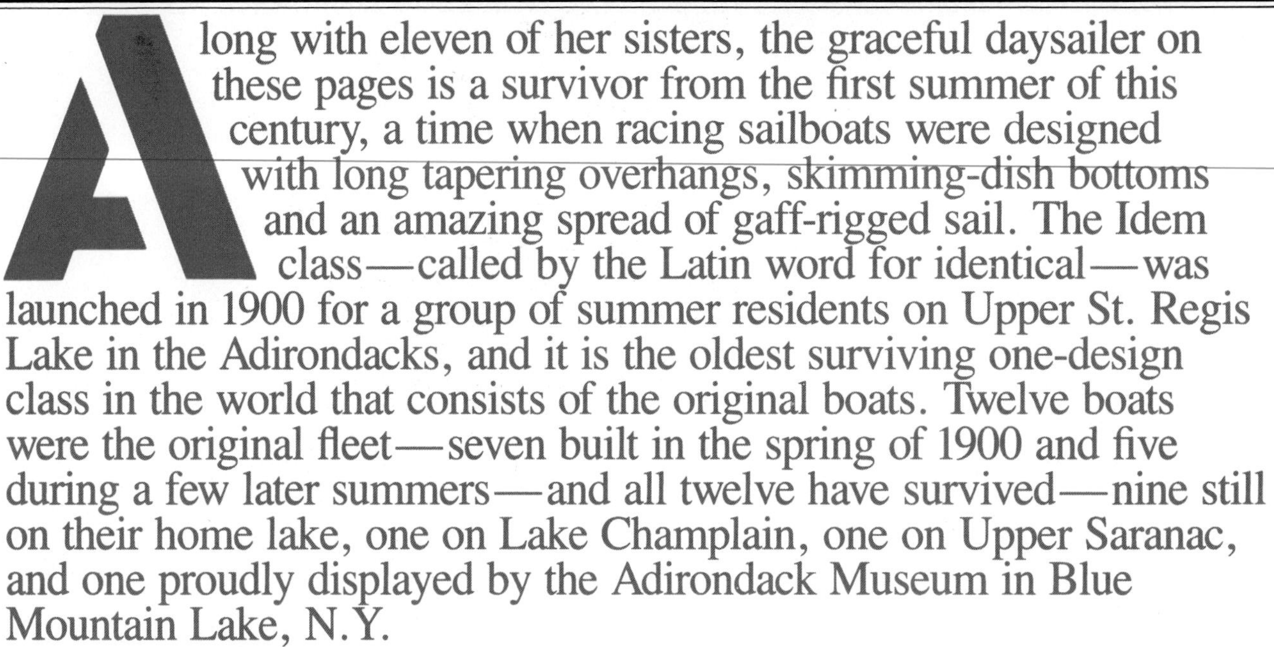

Along with eleven of her sisters, the graceful daysailer on these pages is a survivor from the first summer of this century, a time when racing sailboats were designed with long tapering overhangs, skimming-dish bottoms and an amazing spread of gaff-rigged sail. The Idem class—called by the Latin word for identical—was launched in 1900 for a group of summer residents on Upper St. Regis Lake in the Adirondacks, and it is the oldest surviving one-design class in the world that consists of the original boats. Twelve boats were the original fleet—seven built in the spring of 1900 and five during a few later summers—and all twelve have survived—nine still on their home lake, one on Lake Champlain, one on Upper Saranac, and one proudly displayed by the Adirondack Museum in Blue Mountain Lake, N.Y.

Peek-A-Boo (her original name) was built for Robert W. Stuart as one of the original seven and passed on to several owners before she came to Clark J. Lawrence and his family in the 'thirties. Clark Lawrence's daughter Audrey, now Mrs. Don-Michael Bird of Winnetka, Illinois, inherited the boat in 1972. *Peek-A-Boo* has had a typical Idem history of loving care, occasional unavoidable neglect, and ownership in the same family or among neighbors on the lake. She was stored ashore during World War II, came out of retirement several times in the 'fifties, then went under cover from 1959 to 1968. The Birds have sailed her every season since, except for the summer of 1970 when she was loaned to an Upper St. Regis Lake neighbor, and she was refinished and slightly rebuilt for the 1981 season by Michael Bird and several friends. She is an heirloom, as are most of her sisters.

Clinton Crane designed an outstanding little sloop named *Momo* for Augustus Durkee in 1897, and that summer Durkee brought the boat to his vacation house on Upper St. Regis Lake after she won a Canadian-American challenge on the St. Lawrence. With Crane at the helm, the 20'-waterline *Momo* beat every other boat on the lake, and the idea of a St. Regis one-design class began to be discussed. Crane studied wind conditions on Upper St. Regis Lake in 1899, especially the extreme variations in wind strength at different places on a forest lake full of points, bays and islands, and he came up with a boat that would sail on its ear with fair control, spill wind when hit by a gust, and take advantage of light air with a big spread of medium-aspect sail.

In October of 1899, a circular went out from the St. Regis Yacht Club announcing the Idem at a cost that now seems astonishing: "Members of the Club are hereby notified that an Idem class of jib and mainsail boats will be built for racing during the season of 1900, at a cost of about $750. These boats will be exactly alike and will be raced as a class by themselves without time allowance. The boats will be about 32 feet long, 19 feet water line, and 8 feet beam, with 600 square feet area of sail. A weighted centerboard with a self-bailing cockpit has been decided upon, making the boat non-capsizable."

The Idems were built to Clinton Crane's design and with the dimensions specified, although there proved to be conditions in which they would capsize and spectacularly. When capsized, however, they don't sink altogether. Audrey Bird reports that *Peek-A-Boo,* which leaks a bit after 81 summers, will sink at her mooring if a heavy rain coincides with the absence of a hand or two to bail her out, but she will sink with her decks just under.

The Bird family and other Idem owners enjoy these boats all summer but race them every Tuesday and Saturday in August. The St. Regis Yacht Club also sponsors a Moonlight Race during August, a Handicap Race before Labor Day, and a Labor Day Race in the vicinity of the end-of-the-season weekend. Don-Michael Bird won the Handicap Race among 32 boats in 1978, Michael Bird won the Moonlight Race in the summer of '79, and last season Mrs. Bird and son Michael sailed *Peek-A-Boo* to overall honors in the fleet, including a Labor Day Race with a "hair-raising" thunderstorm that capsized every sailboat on the lake.

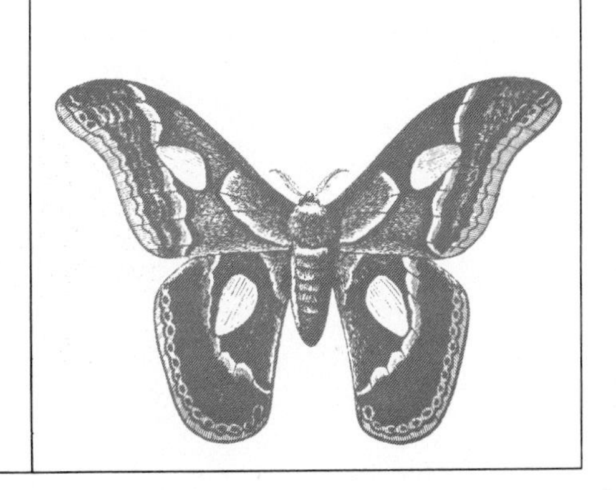

The oldest original surviving one-design class in the world is doing very nicely in its 82nd season, a tribute to an elegant boat well-designed for the waters she sails, and to the special people who have owned them for eight decades. They will be around for many more summers, daysailing, racing, moonlight cruising and—as *Peek-A-Boo* will do this year—defending their laurels.

In America, if the eastern Bering Sea can be called that, just two men can fish an 86′ crab boat. A more normal crew would be four; but on a windy day north of Amak Island we heard a voice on the radio and saw the boat. "We are two, we are two," the voice kept saying, "how many are you?" And then we understood and looked out in amazement at the boat fishing through that heavy weather, just two aboard. The Russians, when the first joint ventures began and American boats were delivering catches to the huge Soviet factory trawlers, couldn't believe how small the American boats and crews were, or how long and hard they worked, or how advanced was their technology, their electronics. American ninety- and hundred-footers were outproducing Russian 250-footers. The Russians even had a word for the American fisherman—"Staliniks," they called them, "men of steel."

ARAB OIL, AMERICAN BOATS, GOD'S FISH

BY JOE UPTON

Esso

We thought nothing of burning a thousand gallons of oil a day. Barely two years later, the fall and winter of the first oil embargo, fishermen like us realized with shock how much we had taken for granted.

Many American fishing boats, especially those built during the last decade, represent the fishing world's state-of-the-art in labor efficiency—vessels and gear super-refined to deliver the most product for the least labor.

The 1970s brought a true revolution to much of the American fishing industry. The popular stereotype of the fisherman, the old salt in the picturesque old boat, became in many places a thing of the past with the 200-mile limit, the explosive growth of Japanese demand for U.S. seafood products, and rapid technological advances in gear and electronics. In harbor after harbor, graceful wooden boats gave way to boxy steel fishing machines.

But efficiency, especially when it exchanges fuel for sweat, can be carried to extremes. Pot fishing, for instance, is generally a fuel-efficient fishery—the pots or traps on the bottom do the actual fishing; the vessels just retrieve them, shuffle the gear around, bring the catch to market. It's a cheap way to catch lobsters, especially when you've got a 30-footer and a Chevy six for an engine. But the fuel-efficiency of pot fishing breaks down when you start pushing a million pounds of boat around with a 399 Caterpillar diesel, an engine about the size of a tractor trailer. On each pot in the king crab fishery, such a boat must come to a complete stop, jockey around, and then accelerate for a quarter-mile or more before stopping for the next one.

Alaska, a fair day, May, 1971—Somewhere in the gray vastness of the Bering Sea we lay beside a Japanese king crab boat for a few minutes, swapping American oilskins for Japanese Suntori Scotch. Theirs was a 90-footer, with the high graceful bow of all their offshore boats; ours was 108′, new, steel. They fished miles of tangle nets set out across the bottom; there were fourteen aboard, the big crew needed to pick the crab from the nets. A very different way of fishing from ours, substituting labor for fuel. The catch rate of the two boats was roughly the same. We laughed at them and their fourteen against our four. We thought nothing of burning a thousand gallons of oil a day. Barely two years later, the fall and winter of the first oil embargo, fishermen like us realized with shock how much we had taken for granted, how vulnerable we were.

In the salmon fishery at that time, the recurring bad dream in my own and many other heads went something like this: it was the "big week"—the time when, after scratching away for expenses all spring and summer, the fish finally arrive in a big spurt and you have a chance to make your season, put a winter's worth of money in your ass pocket, all in a week or so of fast and furious fishing. I headed to the fuel dock along with about fifty other salmon gillnetters. I had all the papers I needed—fish producer's certificate, diesel allocation cards, etc. But one by one all the boats were turned away. "I don't care how many papers you got," the man said, "I'm out, plain out." And we sat at the dock, all of us, and the fish passed by.

Nothing like this ever happened. What did happen—the price rising 50%—was in a way more ominous. Instead of worrying about not getting oil, now we worry about not being able to afford it.

If the U.S. is the Saudi Arabia of coal, then southeastern Alaska is the Saudi Arabia of wood. You could run the entire salmon fleet on wood chips. Through this archipelago of islands—stretching from Glacier Bay, really, down into Washington and Oregon—are the largest remaining stands of virgin softwood timber in the world. In Alaska, my cabin at Point Baker looks out on Sumner Straits. I spotted a log drifting by in the swift tide one day and zipped out in my skiff to put a line on it and tow it home. A firewood log, 5′ thick at the butt, an easy 80′ long, spruce, almost a *year's* firewood in one log! It's like that up there.

So just say that fuel went to ten bucks a gallon, or that the whole Mideast went crazy and no fuel was available; what could you do with wood chips if you really threw some technology at it? In the woodchip-powered steam fishboat, the engine space would have to be substantially enlarged to fit a lot more plumbing and an autofeed mechanism to serve a small, efficient fluidized-bed boiler. Getting dry wood in the rainy Northwest would be a problem; but if you were designing a boat from scratch, you could put hoppers for the chips on either side of the engine space and duct some of the hot exhaust through them, the chips drying in a continuous process before they were burned.

Set up properly, such a boat would be truly independent. With a steam hydraulic saw and chipper set up on deck, you could "fuel up" by laying off a shore, winching beach logs up to the boat, sawing and chipping them, and be on your way. If things really got going, an infrastructure would develop, possibly in the abandoned and ruined settlements along that coast, cutting and drying and chipping wood. You could pull right under the chute and get all the chips you wanted, which would be a lot. Assuming boiler efficiency of 50%—a high figure—a 60′ boat with an efficient hull form would burn something like 300-400 pounds of wood an hour steaming at 9 knots, two or three cords for round-the-clock traveling.

Liquid fuel, compared with this, is incredibly *handy* stuff. If Northwest fishing went the wood-chip route, it probably would be better to trade off the independence of fueling up with raw logs for production of methanol or ethanol from the wood, the liquid fuel to be used in an internal-combustion engine.

Chesapeake Bay, a November morning, chilly, 1970—At six thirty the sky was a pale pink in the east as we loaded beer and ice aboard the 44′ pilothouse-aft trap tender and were soon underway. I was the only white in the crew. The others greeted the day with a good belt of whiskey knocked back with a beer chaser, but I declined. We wound down a narrow creek

Like the South Shore of Long Island, the Jersey Beaches, the Maryland capes and many other places, there once were fish traps along these shores. Now, as far as I could tell, there was only one trapper left.

with farmhouses and summer cottages on each shore, and finally were out on the Bay. In the distance, perhaps two miles away, a gaunt line of stakes marked the water, our fish trap. "Trapping's gone by now," Leroy spoke in a subdued voice, in an odd, almost Elizabethan dialect, hard at first to understand. "Used to be twenty-odd of us, here and across." He pointed across to the Eastern Shore, the Tred Avon River, off towards Cambridge, Oxford, Saint Michaels, Maryland.

A soft-spoken man of fifty, white-whiskered, big-boned, Leroy was the captain. He told me bits and pieces of a life spent on the Bay, of the menhaden boats and how you had to be from a menhaden family before you could even get a job. Of trapping all up and down the Chesapeake from Hampton Roads to the Susquehanna River. Like trapping itself, the black fishermen of the Bay were a culture unto themselves, and ages away from the condominiums and yacht clubs of Annapolis twenty miles to the north. At the trap, we laid the big boat against the pilings. The maze of netting hung from them, about a mile from shore, and the five of us climbed into the beamy work skiff, almost a small barge.

In most fisheries, the fishermen take the net to the fish, using varying amounts of fuel in the process. Fish trapping is the opposite—the net is fixed and the fish travel to it. Here a long leader was strung to the shore, across the route fish so often took when traveling up and down the Bay. The fish, encountering the leader, turn and follow it until they enter the trap itself, a sort of box of netting a hundred feet on a side and with a bottom. Easily entered, the trap is difficult to escape.

Leroy pulled on a line that went down in the dark water until the door to the trap was closed. Then the cold, hard work of "overhauling" it began. Reaching into the water, we all pulled in rhythm, lifting the bottom of the net and slowly working the fish into the corner by the boat. Finally fish were boiling and flipping on the surface, and it was time to brail them aboard with the dip net, a few hundred pounds at a time.

The catch was mostly menhaden—or bunker, or pogies, depending on where you come from. We took about 90 bushels, to be sold for crab bait at $3 a bushel, along with 700 pounds of striped bass at 50¢ a pound. We were back at ten in the morning, and the boat had burned maybe six gallons, a good tradeoff in fuel for the protein harvested.

Like the Japanese tanglenet fishery for king crab, the main input of fish trapping is labor not fuel. It is a method rapidly disappearing from the American scene. Our fishtrap was the only one left in that part of Chesapeake Bay. Of all the others, only stakes remained to entrap unwary sailors at night. And in southeastern Alaska, where presently two or three thousand boats from 65′ on down to rowboats harvest salmon, the entire job used to be done with traps, about fifty of them.

The Alaska traps were a quantum leap beyond anything in Chesapeake Bay. The water was deeper, the tides swifter, the fish stronger and bigger. Traps were enormous affairs, held in place with giant anchors or huge wooden pilings. The companies that owned them kept crews living aboard steam-powered pile-driving barges that did nothing all summer but set pilings. From the point of fuel efficiency, or of fish quality, it was an excellent way to catch salmon. The fish harvested themselves, stayed alive so that the cannery maintained a steady, fresh supply. The biologists, meanwhile, maintained a close count of fish caught.

The fishermen hated the traps. They represented too large an investment for a single fisherman; they employed few men; worst of all, for the Alaskans, they were mostly owned by men in Seattle. So when statehood was finally proclaimed and Alaska had control of its fishery resources, fish traps were one of the first things to go—outlawed. It is hard to conceive of circumstances or even fuel prices that would bring them back.

Penobscot Bay, Maine, June, 1978—The first place I set my floating mackerel trap looked real good—a deep hole inside a point where there was a good eddy to push the fish. It was on the west shore of Vinalhaven Island, by one of maybe a hundred "shag rocks" on the Maine coast, shag being a local word for cormorant. Like the South Shore of Long Island, the Jersey beaches, the Maryland capes and many other places, there once were fish traps along these shores. Now, as far as I could tell, there was only one trapper left.

Afton Farrin, Jr., of South Bristol, is a quiet, almost shy man of about 55. His boat looks as though only the paint is holding it together; his wharf and fish house don't look much better. But year in and year out, Junior, as he is known locally, produces more fish with less fuel than anyone I know. He has two mackerel traps, neither more than a few miles from the town's postcard harbor, and his fish go to the fresh markets in Boston and New York. If it comes right, he can get 50¢ a pound, and many days he is home on his farm by noon. It is a good fishery, and he encouraged me to enter it.

On Vinalhaven, after I had set my heavy anchors to hold the corners of the trap, a local herring fisherman came by to say that the trap would lead herring away from "his" cove. Territoriality is a big part of the herring business in Maine—fishermen will "watch" various coves until a school of fish enters one and, if all goes well, can be netted. A man might "watch" a cove for ten years and never get a fish; but as long as his dory is in the cove it is his.

The next place I set looked even better—a straight stretch of shore with the fish leading in from the ocean. This time I got everything out and set—anchors, kegs, leaders, trap, door lines, etc. And for an hour or so it looked just like it was supposed to. But then the tide began to run in earnest, and the force of it pushed the trap right up to the surface, leaded bottom and all.

The third spot was all that I could ask for—over on the east side of the island, sheltered from the tide, not interfering with anyone else's gear.

Viewed in the perspective of history, the age of the big, oil-fueled draggers will probably prove to be a short one, in some cases not more than the life of a single boat.

And one night I sat on a rock and watched a school of fish making the water fire with phosphorescence. They worked around the point, along the leader, into the trap, just like they were supposed to. But they were brit—sublegal-sized herring. And they were worthless—the mackerel had already passed for the season.

So fish trapping, it turns out, is more than just another net, a different type of gear. It is really a whole way of life, a passive mode of fishing rather than the active mode that so many fishermen are used to. To a person accustomed to having his net on the stern of the boat and steaming around until he finds a school of fish or a good-looking patch of bottom, then towing his net around burning 10 to 50 gallons an hour and more, fish trapping is not an easy switch. Even when a man has a good spot nearby to set a trap, this business of having the net in all the time, having to check it every tide, and taking it out and salting it down in a dory every few weeks in the summer to kill marine growth—it doesn't come easy.

Trawling, or dragging, is the main method of harvesting bottomfish in the world. It is also on its way out. The fish are caught by towing large, wide nets across the bottom of the ocean, a thing that requires big engines and big inputs of fuel.

The "energy crisis," and the big run-up in oil prices, should have come about a decade earlier, for the 1970s enabled many fishermen to finally make an investment they had been talking about for maybe decades—that big new boat. But in the trawling business the big new boat doesn't mean higher productivity unless it can tow a larger net. Many fishermen found themselves with a new boat that towed a 25% larger net but worked with perhaps 100% higher operating costs due to increased fuel consumption and higher mortgages. The result is seen in many New England ports—the newer boats tied up, unable to afford to leave the dock, and the older, paid-for boats still out there slugging away. Decontrol, in late 1980, pushed diesel-fuel prices up over a dollar in many ports. Draggermen who are barely hanging on with dollar-a-gallon fuel will be out of business with two-dollar fuel. It isn't very far away.

There are many ways of catching bottomfish. Scottish seining, for example, is the predominant method of fishing in northern Europe, practiced by graceful double-enders seen in ports from Esbjerg, Denmark to Galway Bay. Scottish seining is an extremely effective way for smaller and generally lower-powered vessels to harvest groundfish. Combined with the Decca navigational system and track plotter (very similar to U.S. Loran C), it enables fishermen to take fish in otherwise inaccessible places with great efficiency.

Imagine a smooth patch of bottom, maybe fifteen acres, all irregularly shaped, surrounded by jagged rock—an impossible spot for a dragger, even though it might be loaded with fish. The Scottish seiner, using the 50′-or-so accuracy of a track plotter, can lay his heavy ropes around the perimeter of the area. They sink to the bottom, and when they are slowly hauled in they travel across the bottom to stir up a mud cloud that "herds" the fish into the small net at the end of the ropes. In many places in the North Sea, boats will actually get in line to wait for a shot at a productive spot like this.

Each time fuel prices take a jump, techniques like Scottish seining become a little more attractive. But this is a much more sophisticated way of fishing than dragging, and fishermen can only make such a change with technical assistance such as a loan of the gear for a learning period and perhaps the advice of a Scottish skipper for a week or so. These are programs which some states, particularly Rhode Island, already have underway.

Viewed in the perspective of history, the age of the big oil-fueled draggers will probably prove to be a short one, in some cases not more than the life of a single boat. New England draggers built in the late 1930s and early 1940s, many of them still in the fishery, went to sea at a time when working sail was rapidly disappearing from the Banks. Only forty or so years later, the imperatives of oil prices, and the inevitability of change it brings, is making commercial sail for fishboats look more and more attractive.

The ironic thing is that many fishermen who are reluctant to change because "it wasn't the way Dad did it," may have had grandfathers who worked on boats like the great schooner *Columbia*, the Gloucester fisherman that drew a crowd at the wharf every time she came home. Captain Ben Pine, who skippered *Gertrude Thebaud* in the International Fisherman's Races, rated *Columbia* a 17½-knot boat "in a good breeze of wind." Or those grandfathers may have been in *Henry Ford*, skippered by Clayton Morrissey, who thought that the 50-mile inshore races never properly tested a fishing schooner, that the true test was the 1100- or 1200-mile thrash home from the Grand Banks in winter. On such a passage, Captain Morrissey was lashed to the wheel, waist deep in solid water, sailing his deep-laden boat on and on for fourteen straight hours.

When Americans think of great sailing boats, it is normally the goldplaters of the Edwardian years and the J-class sloops of the 1930s that come to mind. The dory schooners and the salt-bankers and the mackerel boats that filled the harbors of Gloucester, Provincetown, Lunenberg and other North Atlantic fishing ports for many decades are ignored or perhaps forgotten. But, as far back as the 1880s, designers in New England and Canada's Maritime Provinces were modifying goldplater plans and building boats out of heavier materials for fishing captains who wanted the speed of the Cup defenders with materials that would stand Georges Bank in winter. These boats represented the last stage in a fishing-boat design evolution that began when the first man raised a branch in the wind to carry his catch home faster. Few boats before or since have achieved the

For a few moments the wind came freshening out of the Southwest, and my 16′ sailing salmon-trolling skiff moved smartly through the water. The grace and the lure of sailing and fishing was overwhelming.

power or grace of line and form of the Gloucester schooners. They were great, if not "high," technology.

It is unlikely that sail will ever power a conventional dragger in the future. The power requirements of towing a heavy net over the bottom, and the necessity for fairly precise course keeping (following an "edge" or depth contour, or keeping away from "hangs" that would foul a net), make it a difficult type of gear to combine with sail. It is also unlikely that groundfishermen will ever return to dory fishing with its backbreaking work of manually handling the longline gear.

A more likely scenario for the groundfishery might be the use of "sail-assisted" vessels, using modern forms of passive gear. The Norwegians, among others, have developed longline systems in which much of the work is automated, making possible high productivity with reduced crews. Such a system aboard a modern sailing hull and rig would bring a competitive boat to this fishery.

Ted Hood, of Marblehead, who probably knows as much about 1980s sail, rigging and hull design as anyone in the world, recently designed such a boat. His 96′ "shelterdeck longliner" is probably as innovative and practical a sailing fishboat as any on the drawing boards today. Unfortunately, the run-up in interest rates has prevented this boat from being built. The key to the Hood boat's promise is design work that resulted in a very efficient hull form—one that could travel at 13 knots light or loaded, with very little difference in effort, and with a modern sailplan that combined efficiency with ease of operation. In this case the boat was to be a tall-masted sloop, with four electrically-operated, vertically-reefing sails—two big foresails, a main, and a little so-called "mule" set just forward of the backstay to balance the rig. The boat was engineered to be sailed in most weather from the pilothouse.

Although this particular vessel was designed for swordfishing, it would appear to be soon feasible for the groundfish business, even with lower product prices. The shelterdeck is actually a covered-in maindeck, making the 96-footer a double-deck boat and permitting the crew to work the gear in and out of the weather. The other alternative in a pilothouse-aft boat, as the sloop is, is to have the crew working up on the big bow, an awkward arrangement.

Hood feels that the problem with commercial sail is that there hasn't been any real development work in fifty years. While yacht design and sail and rigging innovation for racing boats have bounded ahead for decades, the diesel engine and cheap fuel since the 1930s have dead-ended commercial sail with the passing of the Gloucester schooners. There is growing interest in it, but few potential buyers to pay for the R&D that has to go into a new hull design plus rigging and sail layouts that can stand commercial use. With just a little help on the R&D, Hood feels that commercial sail will have a strong future.

Point Baker, Sumner Straits, Alaska, July, 1974—For a few moments the wind came freshening out of the Southwest, and my 16′ sailing salmon-trolling skiff moved smartly through the water. The grace and the lure of sailing and fishing was overwhelming. For the first time in years of fishing that spot I could hear the rush of the tide, the soft callings of the phalaropes, little birds like sandpipers. And even a quarter-mile away I could hear the blowing of a humpback whale feeding in the tiderip. "This is it," I thought, "now if a guy could only make a living at it..."

But then, just as I was trying to thread the gear that hung deep in the water behind the boat between a set of invisible underwater peaks that reached almost to the surface, the wind let go. The four-knot tide set me off the "drag." Before I could start the engine, the trolling gear hung up, parted the stainless wire, and the morning's fishing came to an early halt.

The boat was something I had rigged up in the gloomy days of the previous winter when the doomsayers had us all believing that there was to be no fuel next summer. I just sailed and trolled with it that once, but it gave me a clear idea of the limits of sailing and fishing.

My own experience notwithstanding, the Northwest has been a place where the modern sailing fishboat has come off the drawing board and into the fishery. Several conditions provided a favorable climate. First, there was an existing, healthy fishery involving relatively small catches of high-priced fish—the salmon troll fishery. Furthermore, the gear in this fishery made relatively small demands on deck and rigging space, so that sail was compatible. Perhaps most importantly, the prosperity and the nature of the fishery had attracted a number of younger, fairly progressive fishermen who seemed to be willing, or able, to take risks in terms of non-traditional boats that their older and more conservative counterparts would not have.

And Alaska itself, until around 1950, shared with Maryland and its sail-powered oyster dredgers the distinction of having the only sail-powered fisheries. This was the Bristol Bay red salmon fishery, then and now the largest producer of red salmon in the world. In the 'teens and 'twenties, this fishery's full-rigged ships sailed out of San Francisco—three- and four-masters, loaded with Chinese cannery workers, Italian fishermen, American managers, and holds full of empty cans. Once in Alaska, they would lay off the canneries, and from shore the fleets of 32′ double-ended spritsail-rigged gillnetters would be launched to catch the salmon. Until 1950, oar and sail were the only power in that fishery.

In the Pacific salmon troll fishery, the fish are caught on hooks and lines trolled behind the boats. It is a fishery that extends from the California coast all the way up to the so-called "Fairweather grounds," a thousand miles north of Seattle, named for a mountain range and not for the weather. With long offshore passages frequent, and fair winds common, it offered a good chance for the "sail-assisted" boat. Sail-assisted means that the sails are used for traveling rather than for fishing, the problem

J. P. Hartog of San Francisco's Holland Marine Design has produced lines for ten sailing fishboats in various sizes and for various fisheries throughout the world. One of them is *Tiare* discussed in Joe Upton's article; another is a freezer-troller similar to *Tiare* to be built by Blue Bahia in Richmond, CA. The boat shown here is one of Hartog's smaller sailing/fishing vessels, a 41'6" gaff-rigged cutter for crabbing, salmon trolling, longlining and some methods of pot fishing. Three of these little boats are in the works, one in Coos Bay, OR, one in Arcata, CA, and a third in Alaska.

Given the financial climate and general reluctance of bankers to finance something as unknown as a sailing fishboat, the right individual has not yet come up with the $600,000 that a completely set-up boat would cost.

being the need for accurate speed control and positioning when trolling.

There was also a third condition, maybe even a catalyst—Bernie Arthur and Skookum Marine of Port Townsend, Washington. The town, located at the junction of the Strait of Juan de Fuca and Rosario Strait, the beginning of the "inside passage" to Alaska, was a popular winter berth for many salmon trollers. By the time the oil crisis began in late 1973, Skookum Marine had already established itself as a quality builder of salmon boats, primarily the fast smaller gillnetters. But Bernie Arthur had something else—the molds for some very fuel-efficient hulls, sailing hulls in the yacht line that he also produced—a 47′ and a 53′ boat. It was a fortunate combination—the fishing clientele and the sailing molds.

In 1974 a salmon and albacore fisherman finally took the bait and built a sailing troller on the 53′ hull. For the first time, salmon and albacore fishermen could come and look at a boat that might offer a solution to the problem of rising fuel costs. The Skookum 53-footer will pack around 30,000 pounds of fish, and even without sails it operates with 30-40% less consumption than a traditional troller of that length.

Now, seven years after Skookum's first sailing fishboat was launched, the construction of such boats is fully half Bernie Arthur's business. Bernie has been featured on NBC-TV, and has testified before Congressional committees. In 1979, of the ten boats built on the West Coast for sailing and fishing, all were built at Skookum Marine. But it is still slow going. Since the *Sailfisher* was built in 1974 for Ken Short, Skookum has delivered 27 others, mostly 53-footers. Another twelve are in various stages of completion, of which nine will be delivered with sail.

Bernie says that if money were available to the fisherman, he would be selling all he could build. These boats have proved themselves on the basis of fuel efficiency alone. The problem is that many fishermen went to new boats in the 1970s, spurred by booming fish prices and relatively cheap money. Now, when many need a fuel-efficient boat to stay competitive, there is little market for their old boats, and they can't afford the high interest rates.

Bernie Arthur is excited these days about his new 70′ hull. Designed by Ed Monk, as were all his boats, the 70-footer's statistics are impressive—70′ x 18′ x 8′. With a fish-hold capacity of some 80,000 pounds, this boat is a whole new dimension in sailing and fishing, opening up grounds that would be financially impossible for a non-sailing boat or a traditional fishboat hull form.

An example is the "Midway grounds," near Midway Island, in the central Pacific, a 5000-mile passage from Port Townsend. Exploratory fishing has shown the potentially large tuna resource in this area, but the traditional troller simply cannot afford, let alone stow, the amount of fuel needed to operate in such a distant fishery. The bottom line on the Skookum 70 is 7-9 gallons an hour, giving the vessel a tremendous range even without using her sails.

As the near-coast tuna fishery becomes overcrowded, the desire to explore further offshore, to "pioneer" new grounds, becomes stronger. A boat like the Skookum 70, with a blast freezer incorporated into the fish hold, rigged as a staysail schooner, would be able to stay at sea almost indefinitely, following fish all over the Pacific. A full trip of albacore tuna will now bring as much as $80,000 at dockside.

Still, it remains a dream. The first hull was sold fitted out as a yacht, as will be the second. Given the financial climate and general reluctance of bankers to finance something as unknown as a sailing fishboat, the right individual has not yet come up with the $600,000 that a completely set-up boat would cost.

But the "Midway grounds" have attracted other comers, notably the steel ketch *Tiare*, to be launched in the spring of this year and after trials to set out for Midway. Designed by San Francisco naval architect J.P. Hartog, built primarily by George Pell in Richmond, across the Bay, the boat is many of the things a sailing/fishing freezer-processor should be, all packed into 65′ x 15′ x 7′6″. When operational, she will probably be the most technologically advanced of any existing sail-driven fishboat.

Tiare builds on the foundations laid by the current generation of so-called "freezer-trollers." Traditional salmon and albacore trollers ice their fish; as a result, they need to limit their trips to less than two weeks. Another result is that many trips have to be finished before the hold is full. The freezer-troller incorporates a blast freezer into the fish hold (often a modified Thermo King truck-style unit), and its only time constraints are hold space, weather, and fuel capacity. The fish are double-cleaned and glazed at sea; the product is rock-hard and brings a top price. These two-man and occasionally three-man boats have found it worthwhile to run from Alaska to Washington state with a full trip of fish for a better price.

Tiare goes a step further, incorporating the freezer-troller concept into an ocean-ranging ketch with multispecies and multigear capabilities. In addition, in order to keep their large investment productive for as much of the year as possible, George Pell and his partner, Rick Woods, spent a lot of time developing a schedule for the boat, working the peak season in most of *Tiare's* fisheries and getting top price for product delivered.

The circuit they worked out seems to cover much of the Central and North Pacific, with many passages down or across the wind to take advantage of the boat's double-forestay, double-headsail arrangement. *Tiare* would start her season at the Midway grounds with a four-man crew to troll for tuna. Then, working north, the boat would unload the catch in Dutch Harbor, in the desolate Aleutian Islands, where a decade of boom in the king crab fishery has transformed a sleepy Indian town into the largest processing center for seafood (in terms of value) in the entire U.S.

The North Pacific and the approach to the Aleutians will probably make

When all the bugs are worked out, the *Tiare* partners hope for an operation that will gross in the neighborhood of $500,000 a year; they admit that the scheme requires something like half that just to break even.

a good test of all *Tiare's* systems, especially the location of the fish hold, which occupies the entire forward portion of the boat below decks. Weather, tides, and general sea conditions in the Gulf of Alaska are among the worst in the world. The king crab fleet which operates there consists of immensely strong and well-designed vessels, most over a hundred feet, and not a year goes by that one or two isn't lost. Loaded with thirty tons of fish in the forward half of the hull, and running low on fuel and water, the end of a long trip will be the test of the designer's claim that the boat will trim properly at any state of loading. If the calculations are off, the crew would be smart to find another place to sell; the Aleutians are a poor place for a boat down in the bow, even in what passes for summer.

From Dutch the program calls for the boat to proceed to southeastern Alaska, where her crew will buy and process salmon caught by local seiners and gillnetters. The fish would be graded, the valuable eggs or roe separated and processed, and the rest of the fish either sold to local canneries or blast frozen for the Hawaiian restaurant market.

Then, depending on timing and the state of the California salmon troll fishery at the time, the boat would either fish a month or so in that fishery or proceed west directly to Hawaii and the Line Islands, where *Tiare* has a five-month-a-year commitment to catch and process mahimahi, tuna, grouper, spiny lobster and snapper for the restaurant market. In this fishery a native crew may come aboard to supplement the regular crew, enabling the boat to work around the clock trapping, jigging and drift-netting as conditions permit. After five months in Hawaiian waters, the vessel would proceed again to the Midway grounds and the circuit would begin again.

Tiare is perhaps the most advanced sailing-fishing boat in the water, and yet there is nothing really *new*. The boat is a full-bodied traditional design; the rig is that of a masthead ketch, and the fishing technology is already in use aboard other successful boats. What is different is that all of this has been put together in a really ambitious distant-water, multifishery concept.

When all the bugs are worked out, the *Tiare* partners hope for an operation that will gross in the neighborhood of $500,000 a year; they admit that the scheme requires something like half that just to break even. George Pell feels the most important factor in fuel efficiency for a boat like *Tiare* is a crew that will work the sails religiously. He thinks this is the "weak link" in sailing fishboats. And, beyond *Tiare*, Pell and Woods are looking at more advanced technologies that might make fishing sailboats even more cost-effective and efficient. They have formed a fisheries design and consulting company they call Fedco, and they are investigating such lofty technology as rigid and automated foil-type sails of a type the Japanese are experimenting with on a small coastal tanker. In addition, Fedco and Blue Bahia, the yard where *Tiare* was finished, are offering a stock design for a sailing fishboat, along roughly the same lines as *Tiare*, with the buyer's option of either a hard-chine version or a molded version with soft chines and a hollow garboard. The latter is the most fuel-efficient hull; it is also a lot more expensive because of the labor to form the plates.

It may be evident by now that hull form is the single most important factor in the success of fuel-efficient fishboats, sail or power. Nils Lucander, a naval architect from San Perlita, Texas and somewhat of a maverick in the boat-design business, claims that "When man no longer had to row, boat shapes went to hell."

His point seems well taken—that before the development of efficient small engines for boats, hull forms reached levels of slipperiness that have yet to be surpassed. That the Vikings, the Phoenicians, perhaps even Americans like Donald McKay, the Boston clipper-ship designer and builder, developed hull forms far more advanced than anything we are using today.

This kind of reverse evolution can be seen in most harbors. Many of the older vessels, built in the 1930s and before, have a finer, narrower line from the days of heavier and slower engines. Along with the development of lighter, more efficient engines in the 'forties and 'fifties, the predominant hull form for workboats became more and more the "steel shoebox" typified by the beamy, hard-chined boats of the Gulf Coast.

Junior sailing champion of Finland in 1938, Nils Lucander reached Texas and his reputation as a fishboat designer by a circuitous path. Before the yachting boom came to the Great Lakes in the 1960s Nils was one of the few sailboat brokers and dealers in the area; he also began to work on his own sail and motorsailer designs. In 1961, a sailing-yacht owner asked Nils to design a motor yacht that would slip through the water easily and economically, even though diesel fuel was then a nickel a gallon. The result was a wineglass-section double-ender that cruised, then, at a "penny a mile." This boat, launched in 1962, bears a strong resemblance to the fuel-efficient cruisers now appearing on the market.

This experience gave Lucander the beginnings of what has become almost an obsession with fuel efficiency in vessel design, a thing that was to mark him as a maverick, almost a nut, during the days when fuel was cheap. And like most innovators, Lucander has chosen to challenge the conventional wisdom of his profession. Conventional thinking in the displacement-hull design business abides by something called the speed/length ratio and uses the number 1.34 as the s/l ratio that defines "hull-speed." According to this, the hull speed of a displacement boat (the speed beyond which the boat can't be pushed without dramatic increases in power) is 1.34 times the square root of its waterline length.

Nils Lucander believes that the hull-speed "barrier" only exists in the heads of tradition-bound designers, and says that his own boats haven't had a s/l ratio of less than 1.5 in fifteen years. This claim alone has been enough for other naval architects to label Nils a heretic.

At least one tri, a 46-footer homebuilt by Tim Mann, already fishes the distant seamounts... With a restaurant market in Hawaii, and a 12,000-pound fish hold, Mann has a profitable operation where others could not.

"It costs money to make waves," says Lucander. This has been one of his slogans all through the 'seventies—develop hull forms that make fewer waves, and 1.34 becomes meaningless. But change in the fishing business comes hard, and when Lucander moved to the Gulf Coast in 1971 to design workboats and fishing boats, his obsession with fuel and hull efficiency was not shared. *World Peace I*, for instance, was a new 72-footer he designed for a progressive shrimp fleet operator, and when launched she was one of the most efficient trawlers in the world. To design her, Lucander made several trips aboard traditional shrimpers to determine the towing requirements of the gear. To generate the needed 9200-pound bollard pull with the most efficient propulsion package, Lucander specified a Kort nozzle, a controllable-pitch propeller, aft engine location, and a 249-hp engine. The traditional shrimper of the same size would require a 365-hp engine.

Fuel savings with the Lucander designs turned out to be 30% when towing and something like 50% when running free, produced by the propulsion system in combination with an unusually fine hull design that made few waves or wake and had, says the designer, a speed/length ratio of 1.5 when fully loaded. In the fall of 1973, when the Mideast war was beginning, and we were all about to discover what OPEC stood for, Lucander had a booth at the nationwide Fisheries Exposition in New Orleans showing photos and drawings of his *World Peace I*. "Look at that crazy guy! He's got a ring around the propeller and the blades are all loose!" Such was the shrimping community's reaction to Lucander's fresh technology.

World Peace I failed to be the shrimper of the future, and eight years later the entire fishery is almost on its knees, with hundreds of boats unable to fish because of high fuel costs and little prospect for change. Saddled with inefficient—although new—boats, many operators don't have the cash flow to pay for these vessels, much less finance something newer and more efficient like *World Peace I*.

Lucander's work has convinced him that conventional thinking in displacement-hull design is wrong—that it is "special shapes" that determine hull speed rather than wetted surface and waterline length. In the last year or so, with the fall of Iran, decontrol and the rapid run-up in oil prices, Lucander's phone has been ringing a lot more. People aware of him maybe for years, not quite sure what to make of him, are deciding, under the impetus of $1.20-a-gallon diesel, to have a closer look.

A fair hull, an efficient hull, means a "molded" hull, one with compound curves. And because steel, the material of choice for most larger fishboats, is only easily fabricated into developed curves, or curving one direction at once, it means an expensive hull. In a molded hull with a curved chine and a hollow garboard, the steel plates must be actually formed—stretched and forged into shape, a tedious and difficult process. Most boats are built with developed curves, a hard single or double chine—easy to build, but not especially fuel-efficient. There are only a few U.S. yards building molded workboats at the moment, and most of these are large boats, 150′ and up.

But if it hasn't been crossed already, the point at which additional fuel savings can justify the higher initial cost of a molded hull is close at hand. For example, two recent tuna seiners built by Tacoma Boat Company in Washington state were of similar length, but one was hard-chined, the other of molded, soft-chine construction. The hard-chine boat required 7800 hp to steam at 16 knots while the soft-chine version, with 5600 hp, steamed along at 18.5 knots. Once this kind of operating advantage is recognized, and demand is sufficient for "series-built" boats, steel molded boats could be built for a cost perhaps only 10-15% higher than similar hard-chined boats.

Even multihulls will likely have a niche in the fisheries as fuel costs continue to force rethinking of hull, propulsion and gear options for the fisherman who wants to remain in business. A big trimaran, with its fine-lined destroyerlike hulls, can attain steady high sailing speeds impossible for a conventional monohull. And in certain fisheries where the trimaran's drawback of low load-carrying capacity can be balanced by high product value, such a vessel could operate where no other could.

For example, around Hawaii and the Line Islands, seamounts rise from the deep ocean bottom to relatively near the surface, providing a rich habitat for many species of fish. These places are so far from the main islands, however, that fuel costs would make it prohibitive for any conventional fishboat to operate there. At least one tri, a 46-footer home built by Tim Mann, already fishes the distant seamounts. In addition to clipping along in the Trades at 12 knots on no fuel at all, the boat provides an unusually steady working platform, even when anchored in ocean conditions. With a restaurant market in Hawaii and a 12,000-pound fish hold, Mann has a profitable operation where others could not.

Trimaran designer Jim Brown has come up with one of the more unique developments in pleasure or commercial boatbuilding. Urged by Phil Weld, the multihull sailor who won last summer's OSTAR, to produce some designs that would be simpler to build and use in developing countries, Brown worked out a technique for producing hulls that he calls the Constant Camber™ method.

The idea was that instead of building molds to produce components for a single style or size of boat, a mold would be designed and built that would turn out laminated panels with compound curvatures that could be used to construct many sorts of boats, structures, even roofs of houses. The key was a boat design that would be able to use a single panel shape for much of its construction, such as a big tri in which the three hulls and the deck between would all incorporate the same curves. The shape of the

The U.S. fisherman obviously has some hard choices ahead.
The next two years will be brutal, especially in places like the Gulf of Mexico.
A lot of operators in the Gulf will simply go out of business.

panel, by assuming a compound curve, creates a surface which, like an egg stood on end, is incredibly strong by virture of its own shape. A simple and revolutionary idea with many possibilities.

Constant Camber panels are laminated up out of wood strips in a mold to produce almost a pre-stressed skin. The panels, cut to shape, lend themselves to a hull construction in which the strength comes from the design and the skin itself, not from interior framing. The result can be a boat with an unusually high strength-to-weight ratio and with great simplicity of design and construction. Some of the early boats built with this technique are trimarans whose hulls consist of little more than two hull halves glued together, with a deck on top, all out of the same mold, and with no interior framing necessary.

The advantages of this sort of construction, especially in third world countries, are many. The lamination technique allows the use of available and not necessarily marketable woods; construction requires a minimum of sophisticated tools or knowledge; the resultant boat needs little in the way of maintenance. Such light, fast boats, already marketed in this country as SIB boats (an acronym for Small is Beautiful), could have great fishing possibilities in countries where, for instance, an offshore reef protects the shore. Already Jim Brown and his associates, Dick Newick, Chris White and John Marples, have a pilot project going in Africa, turning out Constant Camber panels in a village as sort of a cottage industry. The panels will be used to build catamarans by the local fishermen as well as roofs for their huts.

In 1971, diesel fuel was around a quarter. Now it's a buck and a quarter. Ed Loughlin, energy advisor for the National Marine Fisheries Service, the government's fishing agency, figures it will hit two bucks by 1985 at the outside. You can also hear predictions that it will hit two bucks by the end of this year. There is, by all accounts, a major oil company study that predicts \$120-a-barrel oil, and thus \$5 diesel, by 1990.

The U.S. fisherman obviously has some hard choices ahead. The next two years will be brutal, especially in places like the Gulf of Mexico. A lot of operators in the Gulf will simply go out of business. On top of their own problems of operating costs, they will be competing for the same market with Mexican boats which run on 17¢-a-gallon fuel, and they will probably continue to do so. The smarter fleet operators will manage to keep their heads above water for a while with strategies like operating five months a year instead of twelve, only fishing when there is enough shrimp on the grounds to make it worthwhile. The spectre of "limited entry" in Mexican shrimp grounds will inevitably be raised along with all the outcries it will bring. With 30¢ or even 50¢ fuel, thousands of boats have been roaming the shrimp grounds, but with present fuel prices, boats have to catch more shrimp per boat per trip to stay ahead. Which means fewer boats each bringing in more shrimp.

Technology like the Kort nozzle can keep many of today's boats still operating profitably for a while. The nozzle is one of the few pieces of technology that existing vessels, especially trawlers, can be retrofitted with to substantially, if not dramatically, improve their fuel efficiency. The nozzle, essentially a streamlined, aerodynamically shaped tube around the propeller, is only in the last few years gaining acceptance among U.S. fishermen. The nozzle developed out of the German government's concern about canal bank erosion in the 1920s. An aerodynamic engineer, Ludwig Kort, came up with the short prototype of today's nozzles. Designed simply to reduce prop wash, the Kort nozzle had another feature which was not discovered until a year later. Someone noticed that a 120-hp tug with a Kort nozzle could outpull a 180-hp tug without a nozzle. The shape of the nozzle, especially the wing-shaped cross section, apparently, turned out to generate forward lift, actually sucking the boat ahead.

But beyond the Kort nozzle and other "bolt-on" improvements, probably including more fuel-stingy engines, it seems only a matter of time before many boats built in the 1970s and earlier will be uneconomical to operate on the costly fuel of the 1980s and beyond. By then, demand may be sufficient for molds and designs to be widely built for sailing and other fuel-efficient fishboats. Until then, the fisherman's range of choices will not be wide. Yacht manufacturers will try to convince fishermen that their boats are suitable for all sorts of fishing, that a good racing/cruising sailboat will, with a different deck mold, become an efficient sailing fishboat.

Consider the recent nationwide advertising campaign for the CSY Bottom Line 44 Cutter. "Own a CSY-44 and fish for a very comfortable living!" the ads run, "...If you make as little as one ten-day fishing trip a month, you should be able to pay for the boat and all its expenses, and put as much as \$20,000 a year in your pocket."

The Bottom Line 44 is a CSY-44 hull with a fishing deck mold, and it is advertised as suitable for jigging, longlining, gillnetting, pot fishing, and trawling—although with small nets. If all those claims were true, the CSY Yacht Corporation would be a really fast-growing company. Unfortunately, the ad writers seem to be a little ahead of reality.

Something called the Lancer 44 Multi-Purpose Fishing Vessel is another fin-keel, spade-rudder cruising sailboat hull that has been born again as a fishing boat. There is something of a bandwagon involved with sail-fishing, and many manufacturers are jumping on it. Nils Lucander: "A racing sailboat is, in my opinion, just as suitable for fishing as a Cadillac or a Rolls-Royce is for hauling rocks and gravel."

The problem is that many "cruising" sailboats were also designed with speed in mind, and racing rules have shaped hulls which do not necessarily provide the stable working platforms that fishermen require; for instance, displacement and ballast. A light boat is a fast cruiser, but, to quote Lucander

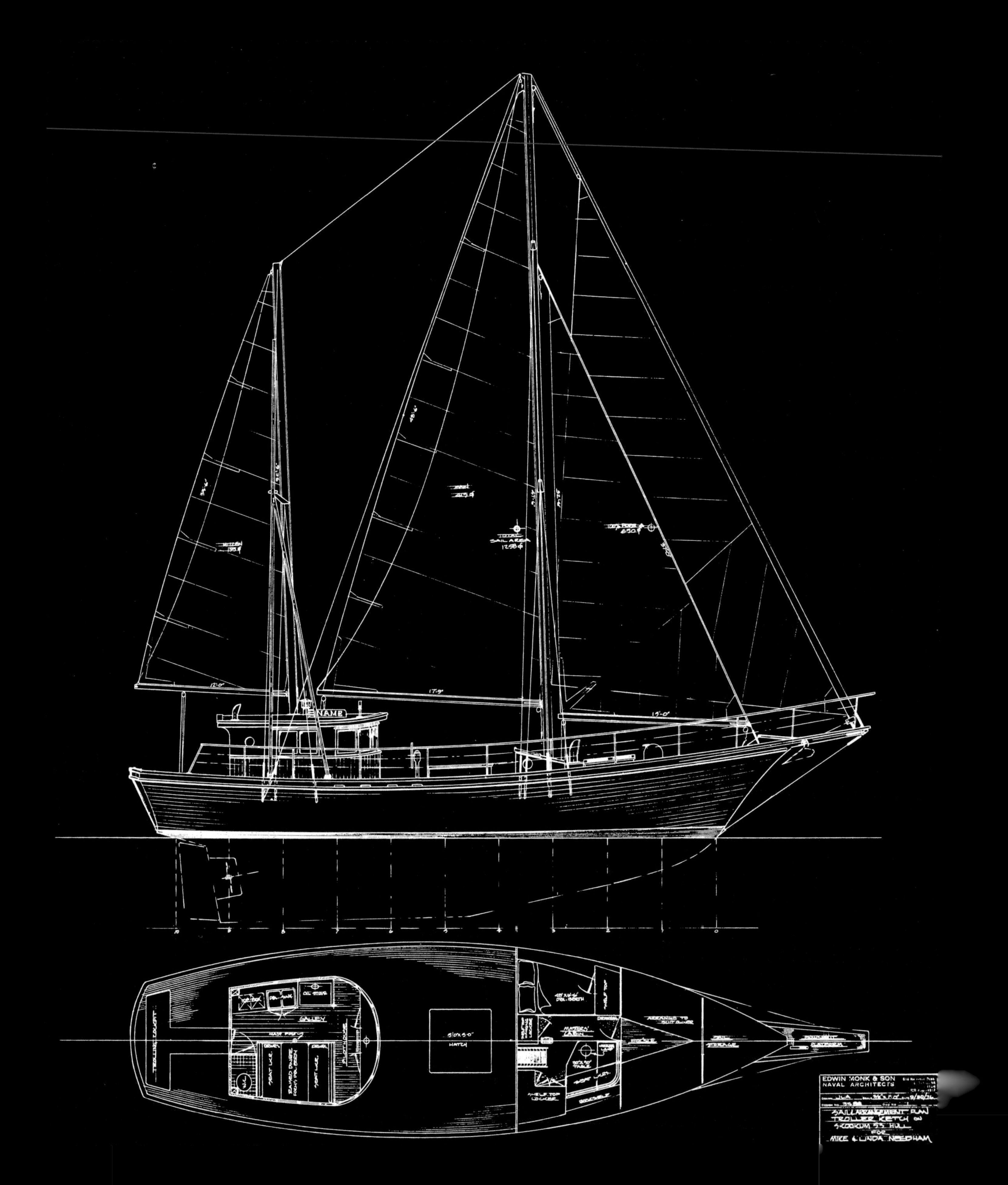
NAME
TOTAL SAIL AREA 1258 ♯
12'-0"
17'-9"
15'-0"
GALLEY
OIL STOVE
HATCH
TROLLING COCKPIT
DBL. BERTH
ARRANGE TO SUIT OWNER
SAIL STORAGE
PLATFORM
EDWIN MONK & SON
NAVAL ARCHITECTS
SAIL ARRANGEMENT PLAN
TROLLER KETCH ON
SKOOKUM 53 HULL
FOR
MIKE & LINDA NEEDHAM

One of Bernie Arthur's Skookum 53 sailing fishboats, *Maverick* was built for Mike and Linda Needham as a salmon-trolling ketch with yacht-fashion liveaboard arrangements designed into her by Edwin Monk. As can be seen, she's a fine floating home as well as an efficient fishing machine that can pack as much as 30,000 pounds of product. Skookum Marine has built 27 sailing fishboats so far, most of them 53-footers like this one, and another nine are being built.

The workhorse of the future's fleets will not be the ubiquitous house-forward, Gulf-built steel 86-footer. It may instead be something like a graceful schooner... reminiscent of the old Gloucester boats.

again: "Only weight can produce both comfort and a stable working platform, to give a vessel an easy, slow motion in the seas. If it is too light, it will tire the crew when working and prevent good sleep when off watch." Fin-keel and spade-rudder boats, especially, should be looked at somewhat skeptically, as this style of hull doesn't have the directional stability for easy course holding that a fishing boat should have.

In comparison to the Lancer and the CSY boats, the Skookum boats, with their full keels and long ballast areas, are probably more suitable for fishing applications. The CSY 44 is a special case, however. For what the company and its President Dr. John Van Ost have done is important—to target a specific fishery with a specific boat. Despite the claims that the CSY 44 is a multigear, multifishery boat, it seems to fit very well into the traditional grouper-snapper fishery in the Gulf of Mexico.

It was a fortunate choice of fishery and boat. This fishery is undergoing the cost squeeze of most other fishing enterprises, and processors and fleet operators, skippers and crews, are looking for a way out of the fuel dilemma. CSY's Bottom Line 44 could be the right boat in the right spot. The grouper-snapper fishery is conducted with electric jigging machines, fairly simple devices that fish single lines and haul the fish to the surface with electric motors. A typical snapper boat of around 50′ uses maybe eight or ten gallons an hour when running and fishes six snapper reels with a crew of three or four. The CSY 44 also fishes six snapper reels and carries a crew of three or four, but it uses two gallons an hour or less.

Dr. Van Ost, originally a dentist from New Jersey, is an unassuming but thoroughly clever businessman. His approach to the Bottom Line 44 reflects his thoughtfulness. He is trying to do in the fishing business what he did in the bareboat charter business in the Bahamas and the Caribbean—combine streamlined management techniques with high-tax-bracket investors looking for tax shelters. When Van Ost began his yacht-charter business in the 1960s, most other charter services were small and slightly haphazard operations. Under Van Ost, CSY established fleets of standardized boats and an efficient operation that quickly got incoming charterers briefed and aboard well-provisioned boats for no-problem vacations. This thoroughness paid off, and now CSY Yacht Corporation has its own shipyard producing a line of excellent cruising sailboats, many of which are bought by investors and leased right back to CSY for use in one of their several bareboat-charter fleets.

For the Bottom Line 44, Van Ost has set up a complete infrastructure system, from an "Academy of Commercial Fishing" to CSY "Fishing Centers" where the investor-owned boats will be based and managed by CSY. The Academy will train neophyte fishing crews in seamanship, fishing operations, electronic aids, basic engine repair, etc. It is a unique setup—the idea is that students spend half their time actually fishing on BL 44's, and live aboard the boats during the six-month training program. The students receive part of the profits from their fishing trips, as does the CSY fishing school. The Academy serves two important functions. First, it is a guarantee to the investor that his boat will be operated by a well-trained crew in an efficient operation, and secondly it is a learning experience for the person who wants to change his game—to buy and fish his own BL 44, perhaps someone who has never fished or even spent much time on the water before.

So, if CSY's Bottom Line 44 is not the perfect boat for every fishery, it is probably good enough for its primary purpose—fishing for grouper and snapper with a minimum expenditure of fuel. And if Van Ost can weather the current economic climate and the usual problems of getting any new venture started, he may be in a good spot to tackle an even bigger problem—the Gulf shrimp fishery, and perhaps the logical next step in sail-fishing, using sail to actually harvest the catch.

Presently, only the Maryland oyster dredgers use sail as motive power for towing heavy gear around the bottom, and they only do it because of conservation restrictions on the use of engines. But in the North Sea, sail draggers once towed groundfish nets, and along the American east and Gulf coasts sailing shrimp boats were productive vessels a few decades ago. Shrimp nets are relatively light, and towed on smooth bottom they might be used under sail again.

What is really happening all over the fishing industry is that each time the price of fuel jumps another notch, another niche opens up in another fishery for an innovative skipper. Fortunately, many fishing operations are still small enough—an individual, a family, a small company—to be innovative.

The cries for a fuel subsidy for fishermen will probably continue to fall upon deaf ears, as will pressures for the government to institute some doomsday technical assistance program to the fisheries. The future, it seems, will be a swiftly accelerated version of the recent past when the big new boats that were the pride of the fleet only a few years before suddenly found the consequences of inefficient hulls and gear types overwhelming.

The evolution of boat and gear design in fishing is about where the creative end of the housing industry was about five years ago, when a single volume could discuss all the low-energy and solar-style houses in the U.S. Today such a work would fill a small library. The broad shape of the change to come will be toward finer, narrower, easily-driven molded hulls, and toward passive rather than active gear. The workhorse of the future's fleets will not be the ubiquitous house-forward, Gulf-built steel 86-footer. It may instead be something like a graceful schooner, with house aft and shelter deck below, reminiscent of the old Gloucester boats but with modern sail technology and fishing gear. Odd blends of tradition and daring have always been characteristic of the fishing business, and such a vessel would be fitting.

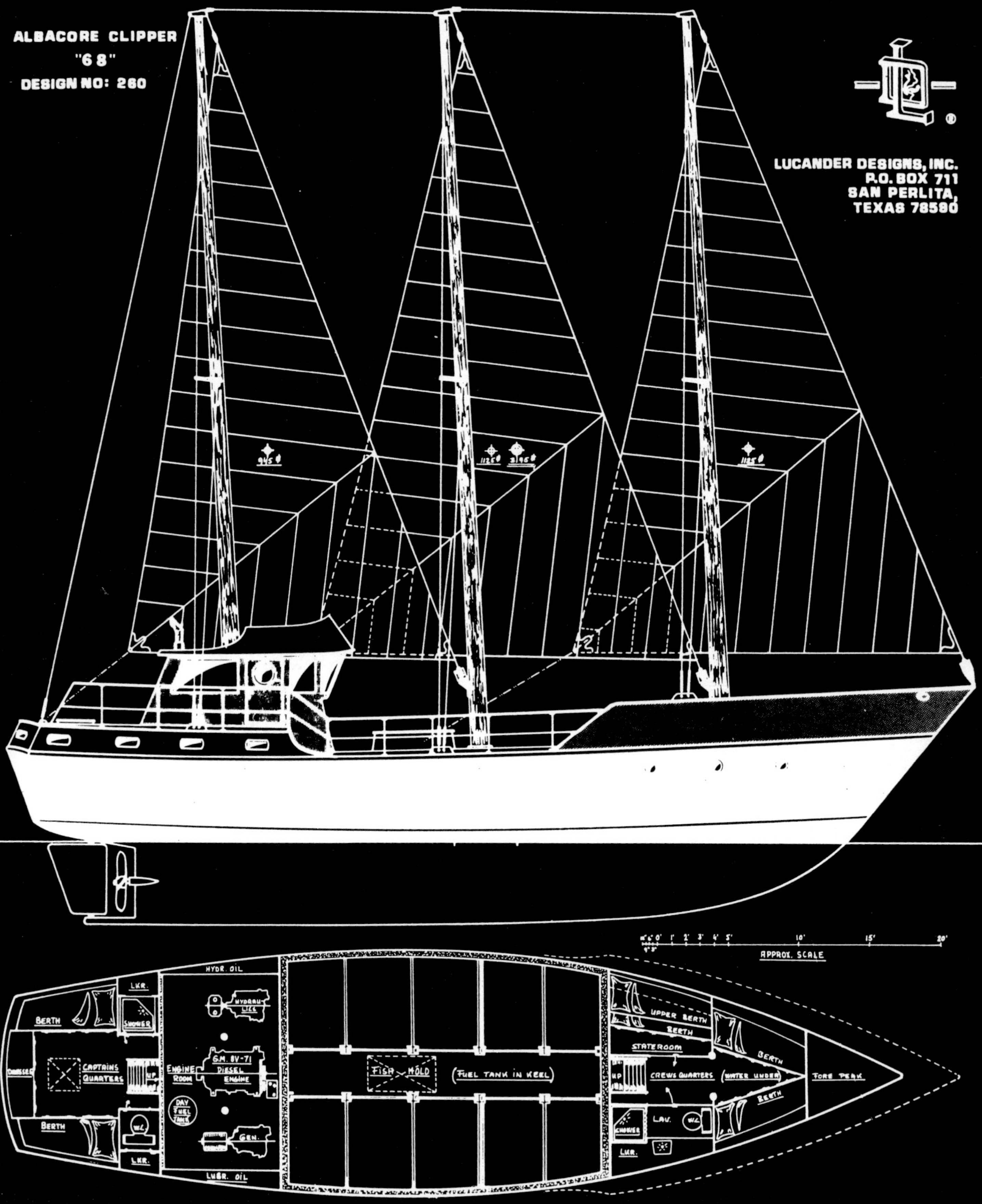

ALBACORE CLIPPER
"68"
DESIGN NO: 260

LUCANDER DESIGNS, INC.
P.O. BOX 711
SAN PERLITA,
TEXAS 78590

Nils Lucander's Albacore Clipper 68 is one of several sailing fishboats he has designed for the bluewater albacore fishery. She spreads 3195 sq. ft. of roller-furling sail and carries a diesel of about 230 hp. The designer estimates that this 68′ schooner will sail at more than nine knots in favorable winds of 15 mph, steam under power at 11 knots, or move to distant fishing grounds under both sail and power with a considerable saving in fuel burned. Her fish holds will take 55,000 pounds of crab, 77,000 pounds of frozen fish or 88,000 pounds of wet fish.

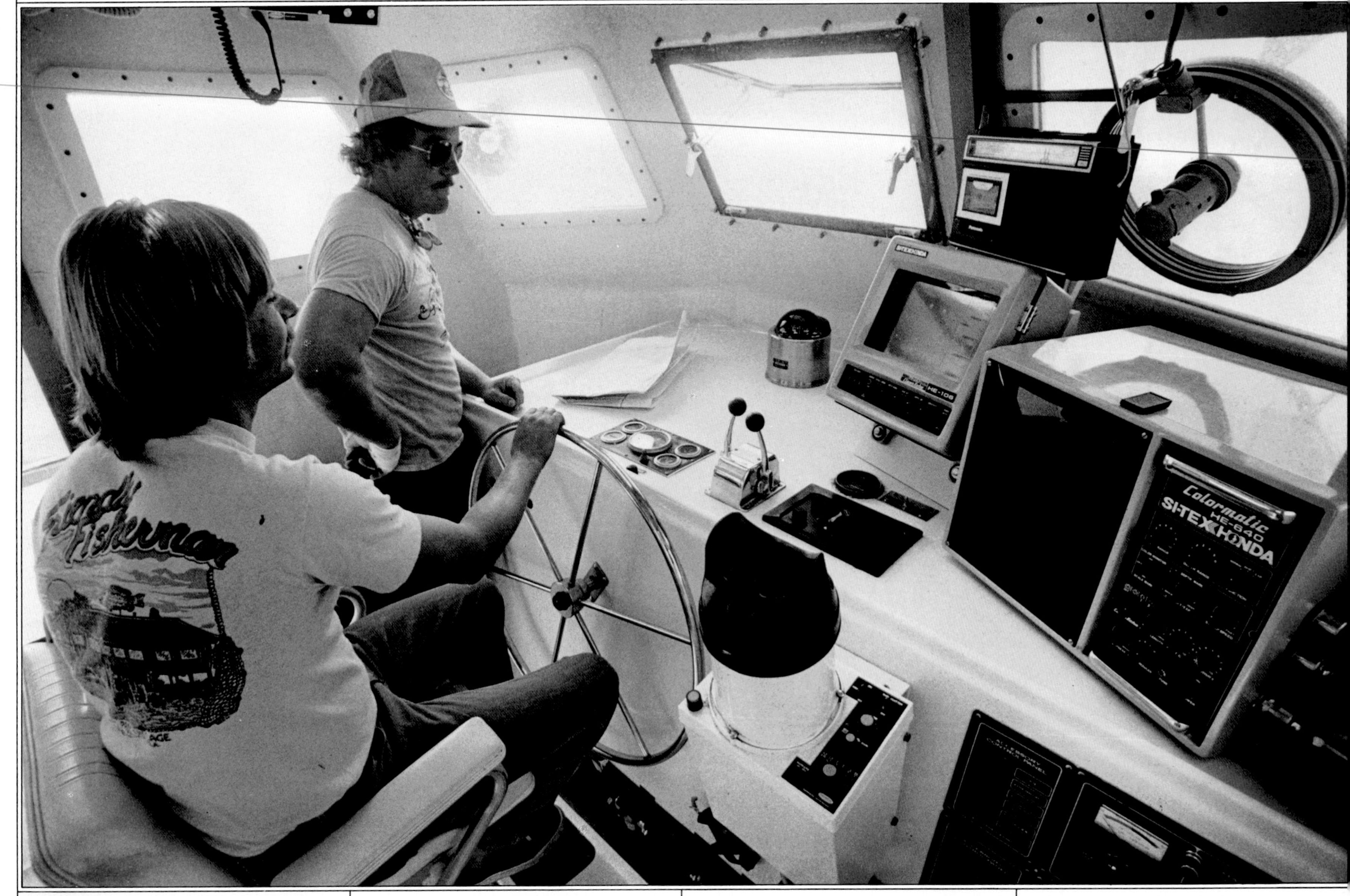

Readers of boating magazines will recognize the Bottom Line 44 as the boat in the ad that says: "Tired of the rat race? Go fishing." She's not the only sailing fishboat on the market, nor the only fishboat that has a yacht hull, but she may be the only sailing fishboat that has an advertising agency.

The Bottom Line 44 is a working adaptation of the CSY Yacht Corporation's 44′ hull, normally built as a cruising sloop in three versions for people whose only thought of fish is inspired by that time-honored cruising question, "What's for dinner?" The time-honored cruising question is one clue to the BL44's purposes. People like to eat fish, and fishing remains a good business for other people who are able to catch trips of fish that deliver dealer prices great enough to cover the increasing costs of going after them, as well as some surplus to cover the fisherman's groceries. (He may not like to eat fish.) A sailing fishboat like this one makes economic sense in certain fisheries.

The CSY Bottom Line 44 shown in action on these pages is one of five similar boats that operate in the grouper and snapper fishery of Florida's West Coast, sailing out of St. Petersburg about 70 miles to bottomfish for a week to two weeks and returning with a trip of iced fish that is sold at dockside to a Clearwater seafood dealer.

A typical ten-day trip for one of these boats might bring back 2000-2500 pounds of fish, of which something like 90% will be grouper, the remainder a mixture of porgy, triggerfish and red snapper. Grouper prices vary between $1 and $1.50 per pound to the fisherman; snapper prices are upwards of $2.30. A typical trip might bring one of these boats $3500, and a 20-trip yearly gross might be $70,000. The five BL44's operated by CSY are all investor-owned, and they employ crews of trainees from CSY's ambitious Academy for Commercial Fishing, headed by Dr. John C. Sainsbury, who directed the School of Fisheries and Marine Technology at the University of Rhode Island before joining CSY. The Academy's trainees go out under the direction of an experienced fisherman/skipper aboard each boat, and the income from their fishing pays back investors in the boats and helps to support the school. Dr. Sainsbury points out that the 2000 to 2500 pounds of fish his students may catch on a typical trip is less than the 3000 to 3500 pounds an experienced commercial crew on a vessel of this capacity might bring back. "If you're using trainees, you don't approach commercial levels of catch," he says. Nevertheless, the enterprise seems to be working. "We're catching some fish, and our catches have been coming up to the price expected," Dr. Sainsbury reports.

The CSY Academy offers an intensive 6-month course in fishing under sail that involves everything from basic seamanship to weather to marine biology. Students pay $1500 tuition, live aboard the boats, and receive a crew share of the value of the catch once returns are made to the school and to the boats' investor-owners. The course is for college-age students and for those investor-owners who may want to fish their own boats.

The program is new, begun just this year, and it is one of those leaps of faith and energy in which Dr. John Van Ost, the man behind CSY (Caribbean Sailing Yachts Ltd.) has something of a track record. Caribbean Sailing Yachts, a giant in the bareboat charter trade, made successful use of a lease-back concept in which owners bought charter yachts and leased them back to the charter company with a fixed rental

BL 44

over a period of seven years, having the use of the yacht for four weeks in the off-season each year and receiving tax benefits from the investment. The CSY sale/lease-back plan for the Bottom Line 44 is a similar program offered to investors who may wish to own a boat that will be fished by CSY's Academy or may want to fish the boat themselves and perhaps live aboard.

The BL44 is built in power and sail versions with the working/living arrangement shown on page 77, and with an economical Perkins 4.236 diesel for power. Ballast is 4000 pounds in the power version, 8000 pounds in the sail version, and the low-aspect cutter rig of the sailing fishboat includes roller-furling gear. Dr. Sainsbury feels that this boat is suited to any longline or gillnet fishery, trolling fisheries and certain of the pot fisheries. She's one answer to the increasing costs of fishing, and perhaps to the rat race as well.

One of five Bottom Line 44s in the fleet of the Academy for Commercial Fishing, with more boats being built. *Ribalov* bottomfishes in the Gulf off St. Petersburg, FL, with baited umbrella rigs on special downriggers from Scandinavia that keep the baits moving with electric power and bring the fish up with electric winches. The catch is 90% grouper, although some hauls include high-priced red snapper. A big refrigerated well amidships holds 11,800 pounds of ice and fish, and catches from trips of a week to two weeks are sold fresh-frozen to a seafood dealer at dockside.

LOA: 44′
LWL: 36′
Beam: 13′ 4″
Draft: 4′11 (power) 6′6″ (sail)
Sail Area: 905 sq. ft.
Power: 85-hp diesel
Hull: Hand-layup fiberglass
Spar: Aluminum
Ballast: 4000 pounds (power) 8000 pounds (sail)
Displacement: 33,000 pounds
Fish Capacity: 11,800 pounds of mixed ice and fish
Fuel: 400 gallons
Water: 200 gallons
Base price: $79,900 (power) $106,585 (sail)
Designer: Peter Schmidt
Builder: CSY Yacht Corp., 5250 W. Tyson Ave., Tampa, FL 33611

RIBALOV
POMPANO BEACH, FL

The CSY Bottom Line 44, one of only a few sailing fishboats on the market, is shown here in action and in cutaway plan form below. The BL44 is available in both sail and power versions, adaptable to several fisheries and designed for crews of from two to four. Consultant to CSY in the development of the boat, and now director of St. Petersburg's Academy for Commercial Fishing, is Dr. John C. Sainsbury, below, formerly director of the School of Fisheries and Marine Technology at the University of Rhode Island.

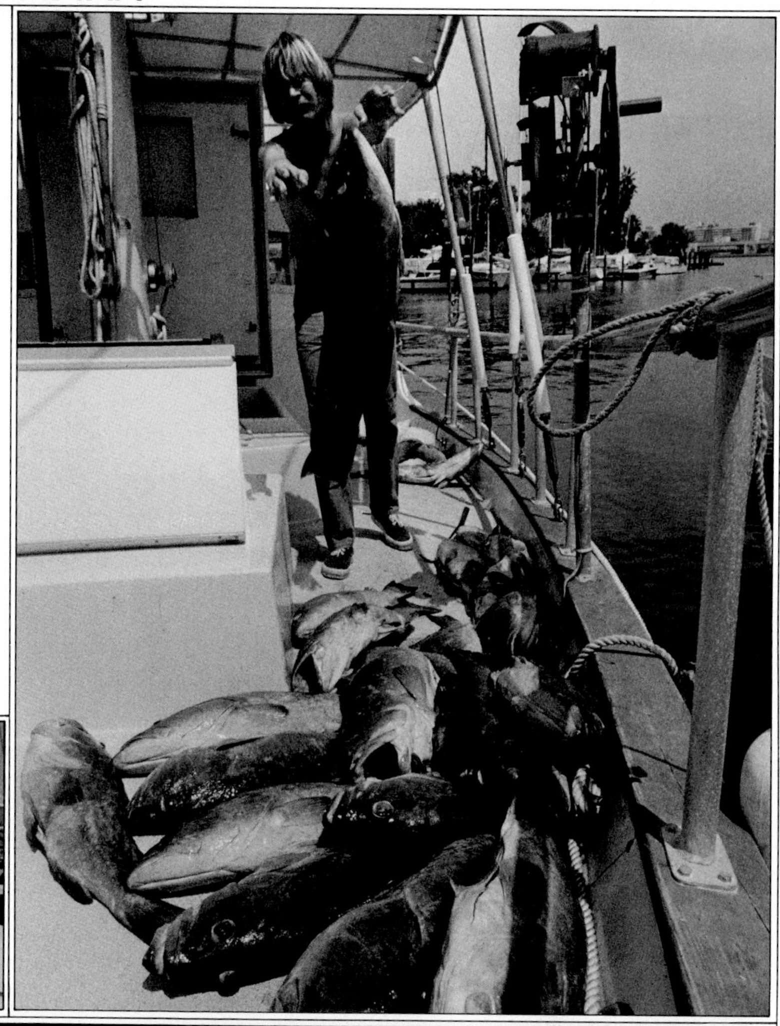

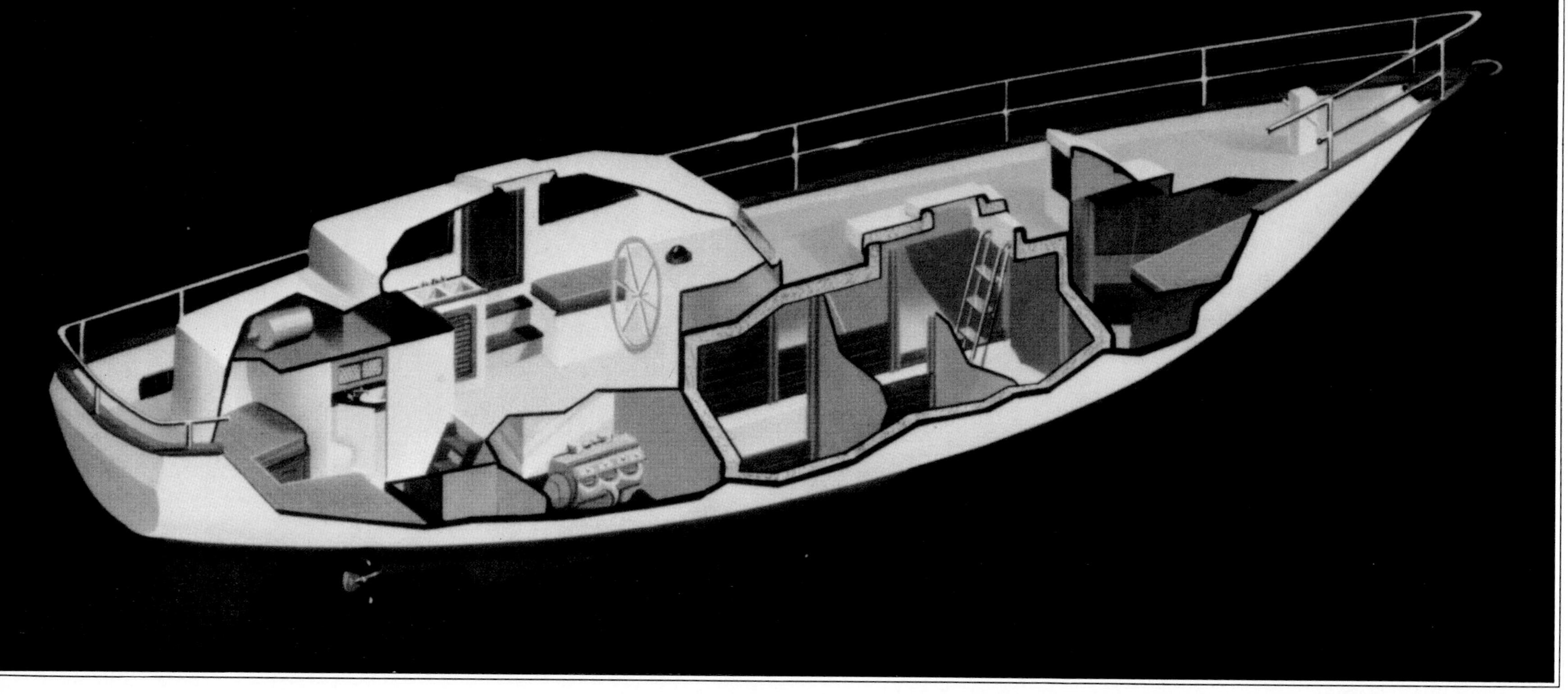

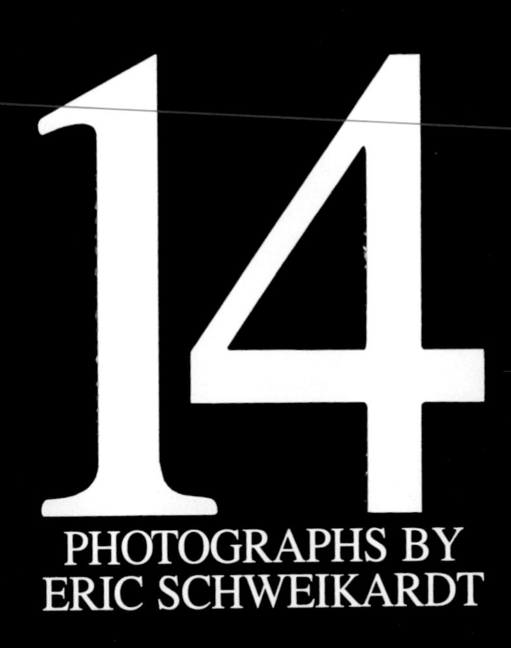

14 PHOTOGRAPHS BY ERIC SCHWEIKARDT

BY MICHAEL LEVITT

The first photograph to appear in Nautical Quarterly, on the issue cover of NQ1, was a bird's-eye view of the 12-Meter *Enterprise* shot from the Goodyear blimp. The water is black; the gray-white sails curve almost sensuously (and seemingly in defiance of printed paper's two dimensions), and two crewmen in bright-red shirts add color, weight, and their thoughts to the weather rail. It is a photograph that works, an image—perhaps a two-hundredth of a second—that summarizes America's Cup racing today: the expensive hours of testing shapes in the tank, the hundreds of hours of drawing-board work by designer Olin Stephens, the thousands of hours of bending, shaping, and welding aluminum, the aerodynamic artistry of the sailmakers, the spirit and sweat of the crew. It is a moment when all the pieces are together.

The photographer in the blimp that day—and under the weight of an impossible number of Nikon cameras, which perhaps accounts for his chronically bad back—was Eric Schweikardt. Not exactly a household name, unless one studies the obscure agate type that gives photographers their credit in the back pages of Sports Illustrated, or remembers the old Life magazine, or buys Schweikardt's successful sailing calendar for a Christmas gift. This winter, when England turns damp and steel gray, this American photographer will be less obscure across the pond as he brings 80 or so of his favorite photographs to that prime meridian of nautical art and scholarship, the National Maritime Museum in Greenwich. The exhibition will run from January to June, 1982. Schweikardt is the first photographer to show work there, as well as the first American to be given the honor of an exhibition.

Who is the man behind the Nikons? Schweikardt is probably the preeminent marine photographer working today—not the best-known, perhaps, but arguably the best. Mustachioed and bespectacled, he looks like the handsome, sensitive member of the Marx Brothers. At age 43, there is a boyish enthusiasm about Schweikardt's life and work, which bubbles to the surface when his shyness isn't looking. "I am really like a kid if things are going right, if I think I'm getting good shots," he says. "I remember in '76, at the start of the Miami-Nassau Race, I was in a helicopter. It was a day when it was blowing hard; the seas were really high; there was bright sunshine on a dark sky. I was so excited, I was screaming when I was taking pictures. It was such a thrill."

After apprenticing with advertising photographers in New York, Schweikardt took his first step into the big time of reportorial photography as an assistant to John Zimmerman, then a staff photographer for the Saturday Evening Post. He recalls a time with Zimmerman, when they were shooting a California politician turned New York lawyer named Richard Nixon. "Nixon came in and spent approximately five minutes with us while we shot him. He tried to make some jokes or something that just didn't work." Four years later, as a young photographer for Life, Schweikardt was covering the born-again Nixon's run for the presidency. "On Sunday night," he recalled, "they had a reception for the press. Nixon came around and had something to say to everybody, or he knew something about their background. Someone said, 'This is Eric Schweikardt of Life.' He shook my hand and said, 'I know you—you were up in my apartment four years ago and took that picture of me.' I mean here I was an assistant, and this was four years ago. I couldn't believe it. I thought this guy has to be all right."

Schweikardt saw his first America's Cup in 1964, while working for Zimmerman. Prior to this, his major nautical experience had been four years on the Weehawken Ferry, in which he crossed the mighty Hudson

"It was a day when it was blowing hard; the seas were really high; there was bright sunshine on a dark sky. I was so excited, I was screaming when I was taking pictures."

twice a day to work as an assistant for the likes of advertising photographers Richard Beatty and Peter D'Mitri.

Said Schweikardt of his first America's Cup: "I was absolutely enthralled by the whole thing. I just kept seeing beautiful things all over the place. An excitement. I just loved being out there." On one of those days in Newport, Zimmerman and his assistant—"schlepper," says Schweikardt—mounted cameras on the towering mast of *American Eagle,* then involved in a life-or-death struggle with *Constellation.* "We put two 250-exposure cameras at the top of the spar. This was before they had radio-controlled cameras, so we made our own by cannibalizing some model airplane radio stuff. Before going out, there's a guy working near the top of the mast. All of a sudden he calls down, 'Hey, are these cameras supposed to be going off up here?' Some taxi radio or garage-door opener had set them off. We got 500 beautiful photographs of the boat tied up to the dock."

Zimmerman introduced Schweikardt to Buddy Bloodgood, assistant picture editor of Sports Illustrated, whose only encouragement was to keep in touch. In 1965, while in Detroit with Zimmerman shooting the new Detroit cars—then a subject of some interest—Schweikardt called Bloodgood at S.I. Bloodgood said that as long as he was there he might take a picture of the new Corvair. Opportunity knocked. Schweikardt approached Zimmerman for spiritual solace as well as the loan of equipment. "John told me, 'You can handle it.' I had to borrow a camera and lens from him because I didn't have any equipment there. But I did it. I probably shot five or six rolls of the car at the GM Test Track." The picture ran in black-and-white across one thin 13-pica column of Sports Illustrated, but it was the beginning of the big time.

Schweikardt put in seven years working as an assistant for various photographers. Did he feel like a slave during this lengthy apprenticeship? "No, I never did, although I suspect it's easy to get that feeling. I just felt that I was learning a lot. To me this was my education...John taught me an awful lot. He was a good teacher. He wasn't afraid that I was going to steal his secrets. I was also getting to meet some of my heroes."

One such hero was Gordon Parks, the multitalented black man who was a contract photographer for Life. Parks published books of poetry, composed music played by the Vienna Symphony Orchestra, wrote a book called *The Learning Tree* and later wrote and directed the movie "Shaft." "Just a marvelous man," says Schweikardt. "His face looks like a map of the world. I go through fits of depression every once in a while...You know, you feel like you're standing still and can't get a good creative thought. I was going through one of these once, and I went to see a Gordon Parks exhibit in the reception area at Life. He had huge color prints on display there, and in the background was his music. They had his poetry all over the place. I can remember just going there and having tears in my eyes, thinking how terrific this is. I was standing and looking at one of his pictures—it was a pigeon against a blue shadow on the sidewalk. I must have stood looking at it for an hour. All of a sudden a voice from behind me said, 'What do you think of that picture? You've been looking at it for a long time.' It was Gordon Parks. We started talking. He said, 'Let's go downstairs and have a cup of coffee.' He spent quite a while with me. I came away thinking I could lick the world."

One day the Sports Illustrated picture editor approached him about photographing an attempt to set the land-speed record in a jet-powered automobile on the Bonneville Salt Flats in Utah. He said it was to be a big color spread and asked if Schweikardt thought he could handle it. "Put me in, Coach," recalled Schweikardt with a laugh.

The rocket-car was expected to break 600 mph, and Schweikardt and his assistants dared not get within a quarter-mile of the course. They lined the track with cameras which would fire by remote control as the projectile made its dash down the Flats. Schweikardt was poised at the end in a helicopter to photograph the moment when the parachute would pop out to slow the car. "We're up there, waiting and waiting. The pilot says, 'I'm going to have to set it down. We're running out of fuel.' I said, 'Just a minute.' And way in the distance we see this dust storm tearing down the black line. I'm shooting and all of a sudden all hell breaks loose. The car goes end-over-end and flames break out. A tire came off and damn near went through the helicopter. We set down alongside, and I'm taking pictures all the time. The driver's moaning and he's covered with blood. I couldn't believe he was still alive. He's pinned in what's left of the car. We tore off a strut from the helicopter and used it as a crowbar, trying to get him out. All of a sudden he looks up and says, 'Take your time, fellas. I'm O.K.' He'd just crashed at 618 mph. We flew him to the hospital; they gave him a shower, washed the salt off him, and released him."

Schweikardt's assistant flew the undeveloped film back to New York, and the next day the photographer called the magazine to find out how it came out. "They told me it looked super and it was running for five pages. I said, 'I can't wait to get back there and see it. I'll take the next flight out.' They said, 'No! Why don't you go on to Brigham Young and shoot a football game,' and then go someplace else to shoot something else. I thought it's happened." When he got back to New York, S.I.'s picture editor took him to lunch and put him under contract.

Schweikardt covered the '67 America's Cup for S.I. Speaking of that experience, he said, "I thought it was great being out there in the salt air and the sun, even if it was the America's Cup and the Coast Guard wouldn't let you get close enough to get anything worthwhile." His next nautical assignment was the Bermuda Race. Following the start in Newport, he flew to Bermuda to record the finish. There, from a small boat, he took spectacular photographs between near-terminal bouts of

"When you're surfing a 79′ boat, that's a thrill. We went over 21 knots. The guys were all screaming. Remember that surfing expression *stoked?* Well, everybody was stoked."

seasickness. He still knew nothing about sailing, although he'd mastered a fair bit of the literature on seasickness. "When I started out, I was just recording what was happening. It took a while to get it because you think if the boats were somehow going the other way, the light would be so much better, but then you find out the boats can't go that way."

In 1971, Schweikardt learned to sail at Club Med in Martinique with his friend Jim Kearns and their wives. At the end of the week, two races were scheduled. "We thought we'd jazz it up a little, and so we got matching team uniforms," he recalls. "We jogged down to the boat and did calisthenics. Everyone was watching and wondering who are these people?" They won both races by sizable margins. The next week Schweikardt and the same crew went to Annapolis to charter a boat. "The following week Jimmy and I decided we were going to buy a boat. We had no idea what kind of boat to buy because we didn't know anything about them. But when we were in Annapolis we wandered the docks, and there seemed to be a lot of Cal 25s around. We came across this guy who was sitting in the cockpit of one drinking a beer. He looked like he owned the world. We started talking to him, and he said that the Cal 25 is the 'finest kind.' We believed him." The next week they saw a Cal 25 advertised for sale in Boston, and they flew up and bought it.

Schweikardt, unimpressed with his and his friend's week and a half of sailing experience, implored Hugh Whall, then the boating writer at Sports Illustrated, to help deliver the boat to Connecticut. The week before the delivery, Whall was racing a powerboat with Dr. Bob Magoon off Point Pleasant, N.J. "They spun out," Schweikardt remembers. "I was right above them in a helicopter. I shot the whole thing. They weren't moving; I thought they were dead. We had to take Hugh to the hospital. He broke a bunch of ribs and damaged his kidneys." While Whall was convalescing, Schweikardt peppered him with questions about how to cruise in a small boat. "I kept Hugh up for the next three nights drawing me diagrams...'How do you put up a spinnaker? How do you know where you are? How do you avoid ships?' He was marvelously patient with me."

Schweikardt and Jim Kearns left Cohasset early one morning heading for the Cape Cod Canal. It was one of those days. "God, we had a following breeze. I said to Jimmy, 'Do we dare try a spinnaker?'" They consulted one of Hugh Whall's drawings. "We hoisted it, and the thing just blossomed. Perfect. I've never been able to do it like that since.".

The next day a thick fog descended and Schweikardt and Kearns headed for the shores of Buzzards Bay. "We were in amongst a couple of boats, surrounded by beautiful large homes. We were waiting out the fog and having a second cup of coffee. Suddenly a beautiful woman comes out of one of the houses followed by a romping dog. She takes off her clothes and goes swimming. She isn't 25 yards from us. Jimmy and I are fighting over the binoculars. It was wonderful. We didn't say a word. She didn't know we were there. She got out of the water, dried herself off, and then just wandered around the yard for a few minutes. We thought this was what sailing was all about. We tried to find out who she was so we could send her some roses."

Schweikardt's idyllic introduction to cruising under sail was followed by some equally powerful experiences racing under sail. It was aboard the maxi *Kialoa III* that he would find himself among the giants of ocean racing and take some of his most magnificent photographs. He recalled what it was like when he first sailed aboard her during the '75 SORC. "I'd never been on a boat that size. When we first started out, it seemed like there were pictures everywhere. So much is happening on that boat. My God, there are 18 or 20 guys on the crew. We got hit by a squall shortly after the start. We blew out a chute. That one was down and a new one up 20 seconds later. And that spinnaker costs as much as my boat. Sometimes these things are happening, and it's sort of frustrating not to be getting it all on film.

"I remember coming down from Ft. Lauderdale to Miami at night. I wasn't taking pictures so I took a turn on watch. We had up a spinnaker, a mizzen spinnaker and staysail—about 10,000 square feet of sail. And we're surfing. And when you're surfing a 79′ boat, that's a thrill. We went over 21 knots. The guys are all screaming. Remember that surfing expression *stoked?* Well, everybody was stoked..."

Six months after signing on with Sports Illustrated, a message came that Dick Pollard had called. "I had no idea who he was," says Schweikardt, "but I knew from the phone number that he was with Time/Life. Told Pollard was the photo editor at Life, Schweikardt returned the call. They met. "He said to me, 'How come you've never come up to see me?' I mean here I am talking to the man from Life—working there was everyone's dream if you were any kind of photographer. I said, 'I didn't think I had anything to show you.' He said, 'I've been following your work...' I just sort of walked out his window on the 29th floor and didn't touch ground. I was 29 years old, and here I had a combination Life and Sports Illustrated contract."

The marine images on the following pages are a few examples of what people like Life's Dick Pollard saw when they looked long and hard at Eric Schweikardt's photographs. Competent photographers are able to frame a good image; good photographers are able to make that image sharp; excellent photographers are able to orchestrate lively color qualities from the complexities of Kodachrome film and the moment's light; superb photographers are able to bring their photographs just a bit more. These photographs have that extra something—in some the aura of a moment frozen, in others a face that's looking right at you, in places a crisp reality that remains exquisite and mysterious. These photographs have it, whatever it is. Enjoy them.

Austra-*lia*, Alan Bond's America's Cup entry in 1977 and again in '80, celebrates an early Trials victory over *France* by surfing into Newport in this '77 photo. Schweikardt recalls the joy of the crew at the not-unexpected win and the sheer exhilaration of that moment when 30 tons of aluminum and lead behaves more like a bird than a boat: "The crew was hooting and hollering when surfing down those waves." On the following spread, *Enterprise* has a photographic moment of glory while sailing away from Old Glory. Her moments of glory were more aesthetic than athletic as *Courageous* went on to defend the Cup that year. Said Schweikardt about this photograph: "I remember thinking that someday I'm going to need a narrow horizontal and this is perfect." We agree.

12
US 27

C*lipper's* kiddy corps poses for the photographer, this day dangling from a helicopter. The shot is a setup, taken as part of an advertising campaign for a shirt manufacturer who equipped the crews. For a news photographer—the shirt Schweikardt usually wears—such setups can be luxurious; the photographer is in direct contact with the subjects, not reacting but choreographing. Aerial photographs are a distinct part of the Schweikardt style. This angle eliminates the distracting horizon line and seems to dramatize the action on boats, especially racing boats.

T

he pho-
pher sits
ad Ted
er to record
eavy upwind
n on
cious, taken
g the '78
ont series,
h just pre-
s the

Bermuda Race. It was blowing a gale, Schweikardt recalls, "however, it was one of those unusual days that was sunny and clear, and yet had winds like that." On the next spread is the Frers maxi *Bumblebee 4* as

seen in this year's SORC. Schweikardt was distracted for this one from photographing *Kialoa* for Sports Illustrated. "When I see something like that, I just can't resist it," he said.

bumblebee 4
C.Y.C.A
SYDNEY

A crew member runs a reef line on Mike Swerdlow's *Aries* in the '76 Miami-Nassau Race at left. Said Schweikardt of this day: "I was so excited, I was screaming when I was taking pictures. It was such a thrill." A more serene moment, above, is this trimaran anchored in French Polynesia. At right is Dr. Bob Magoon's Cigarette 39 race boat blasting over the blue-green waters of the Bahamas.

At left is *Acadia* in the Nassau Cup Race with another competitor breathing down her neck. Above is the charter boat *Shenandoah*. Schweikardt was on the Castle Hill lighthouse—which guards Narragansett Bay—"trying to get pictures of a pretty sunset when, by God, this boat comes in as if I'd planned it." At right is *Kialoa*, Jim Kilroy's latest maxi. An angle like this is enough to make skeptics believe in the Bernoulli principle.

At left, *St. Francis VII* is seen during the Six Meter Challenge Cup in '79. Above, this haunting image comes from Pangnirtung, on Baffin Island, just inches from the Arctic Circle. Schweikardt was there to shoot an ad for a liquor company. Two weeks of waiting for the weather to clear—in a settlement which offered but two 10-year-old National Geographics for entertainment—gave him time to bring back pictures like this. Right, from this height, racing legalisms like "mast abeam" or "weather boat keep clear" are meaningless. Five boats add shape and much beauty to a near-calm sea.

John Andresen's *Ecila* steams along in the Florida Keys in the photo below, and the man himself poses on the foredeck at right. *Ecila* is a new Amapala 35, built in Honduras of cold molded Honduras mahogany and powered by twin Chrysler Mitsubishi diesels for a combination of high cruising speed and low fuel consumption. The photos on these pages show some of the fine joinerwork in teak and rosewood that distinguishes these boats built in a place where wood craftsmanship is still the standard.

Amapala is the name of a town on an island called El Tigre on the west coast of Honduras. This boat and a similar 40-footer are built there by John Newton, the man who founded Grand Banks more than 20 years ago in Hong Kong, and Amapala's operation is similar in concept to the Newton family's enterprises in the Far East. The concept is to build a high-quality wood boat in a place that combines fine boatbuilding wood, skilled hand craftsmen and a favorable economic climate. The result, as customers for Grand Banks trawler-type yachts discovered two decades ago, is a lot of boat for the money. The Amapala 35, a twin-diesel sportfisherman of lightweight cold-molded wood, is priced at only $80,000 as this is written, $70,400 with 330-hp Chrysler gas engines. She compares favorably in looks, performance and equipment to semi-custom sportfishing boats that sell for three times that amount and more. The 40-footer is priced at about $95,000 with gas engines and $120,000 with twin Cat diesels.

Newton has built 32 of the 35-footers and a dozen of the 40s since 1979, and most of them have been sold on the U.S. West Coast under the name Pacific Bluefin. Mike Balfe of Merrill-Stevens in Miami, the East Coast importer of these boats under the Amapala name, says that he could sell twice as many as he's been selling if only he could get John Newton to build them faster.

AMAPALA 35

But Newton's plant in Honduras is old-fashioned in attitude if not in technology, and it is expected that only 12-15 Amapala boats will be built in 1981.

Hulls are constructed of four skins of solid Honduras mahogany over Honduras mahogany frames, cold-molded with epoxy resin into a single structure, with a final covering of fiberglass cloth and linear polyurethane finish. Bottom thickness is greater than 1″. Trim and cockpit sole are solid teak, and both teak and rosewood are used extensively below decks for furniture, cabinetwork and trim. Both Amapala hulls were designed by San Diego naval architect Lawrence Drake, and their design and construction are similar to the Drake Craft boats the designer built on the West Coast between 1953 and 1969. "John Newton knew of my construction techniques," says Drake, "and I guess he liked what he saw. He wanted me to design these boats for the same kind of cold-molded boatbuilding." One advantage of cold-molded wood is its light weight combined with structural strength. The Amapala 35 has a full-load displacement of 17,671 pounds, and her lightness, combined with a conventional vee bottom that has 6° deadrise at the transom, makes her amazingly easy on fuel. The owner of the boat shown here reports that he used 55 gallons of diesel on a recent hundred-mile, 7-hour run down the Florida coast. John Andresen, owner of *Ecila,* is pleased and a bit surprised by his boat's combination of flashy performance and fuel economy. "She performs beautifully," he says. "I know she's making better than 19 knots very efficiently, and I've had her up as high as 25."

The 40′ Amapala is reported to deliver 1.03 nautical miles per gallon at a cruising speed just under 20 knots, and to troll at 6 knots while covering 2.1 nautical miles per gallon. Both hulls, as these few photos indicate, are easy-running vee-bottom types, with vee sections the designer describes as "kind of semi-warped," and with a fine entry, extreme deadrise forward, nearly flat sections along the chines for lift, and a relatively deep keel line for good tracking. Styling is clean and simple, an

The plan below right shows one of several simple, efficient arrangements for the 35′ Amapala, and photos above right show a few details. John Andresen's boat has a folding table and bench seat in place of the dinette shown in the plan, and by next season she promises to be bristling with outriggers and other billfishing hardware for an angling season in the Gulf Stream and cruising the Gulf Coast from a base at the Key Largo Angler's Club. She represents not only an economical boat for the fuel-costly 1980s but a first-cost bargain at $80,000.

LOA: 34′11″
LWL: 31′2″
Beam: 13′10″
Draft: 2′3″
Hull: Cold-molded Honduras mahogany, fiberglassed
Displacement: 17,671 pounds at full load
Power: Twin 330-hp gas engines or 200-hp diesels
Fuel: 300 gallons
Water: 89 gallons
Designer: Lawrence Drake
Builder: Amapala Yachts
Base Price: $70,400
Importer: Merrill-Stevens, 2640 S. Bayshore Dr., Miami, FL 33133

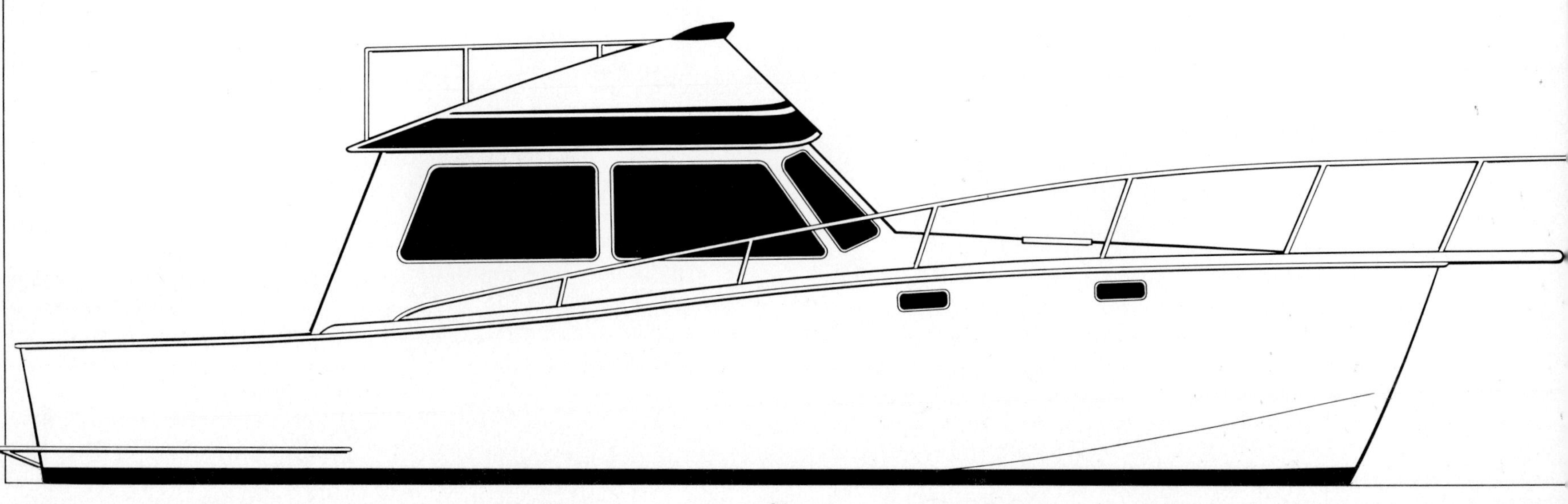

all-business boat with no folderol.

Standard power for the Amapala 35 is a pair of Chrysler Mitsubishi diesels rated for 200 hp each. The 40's standard diesels are twin Caterpillar 3208T engines rated for 251 shaft hp. The equipment list for both boats is unusually complete, and includes such niceties as a trim-tab system; bronze struts, shaft logs and exhaust tips; stainless-steel rails on foredeck and flying bridge; a transom door in the cockpit; a removable instrument console on the bridge with cabinets to hold 73 cubic feet of gear.

The 35's arrangement plan is simple and efficient, with a long galley console in the deckhouse opposite a dinette and stowage locker, or as in *Ecila* a combination of dining table and upholstered bench seat. Below is a generous head with shower, a big double berth to starboard, and a pair of vee berths forward with two hanging lockers. Lavish amounts of rosewood are used in the deckhouse and below, even to a rosewood facing for the refrigerator. The four-burner stove is LP gas, and the double sink is served with engine-heated hot water.

Hulls are constructed of four skins of solid Honduras mahogany over Honduras mahogany frames, cold-molded with epoxy resin into a single structure, with a final covering of fiberglass cloth and linear polyurethane . . .

Aft is an 80-sq.-ft. cockpit with teak sole and trim, and above is a like-sized flying bridge with cushioned seats for eight.

John Andresen keeps his Amapala 35 at the Key Largo Angler's Club, and his plans for the next winter season include a full arsenal of billfishing gear that his son, Advertising Manager of Saltwater Sportsman Magazine, has talked him into. "We'll use her next season exclusively for offshore fishing for billfish," he says. "She'll be rigged with everything—outriggers, bait wells, the whole bit." John Andresen and his wife Lally plan to do some southern cruising as well, around Florida Bay and up the Gulf Coast, perhaps as far as Texas.

John Andresen was a sailor until he retired from business ten years ago. He's had four powerboats since then, three of them built by Huckins and the fourth a custom-built sportfisherman designed by Alan McInnis. He's an experienced sport-fishing skipper, and his choice of this boat represents a very well-informed decision. He feels she's not only a great boat but a great bargain.

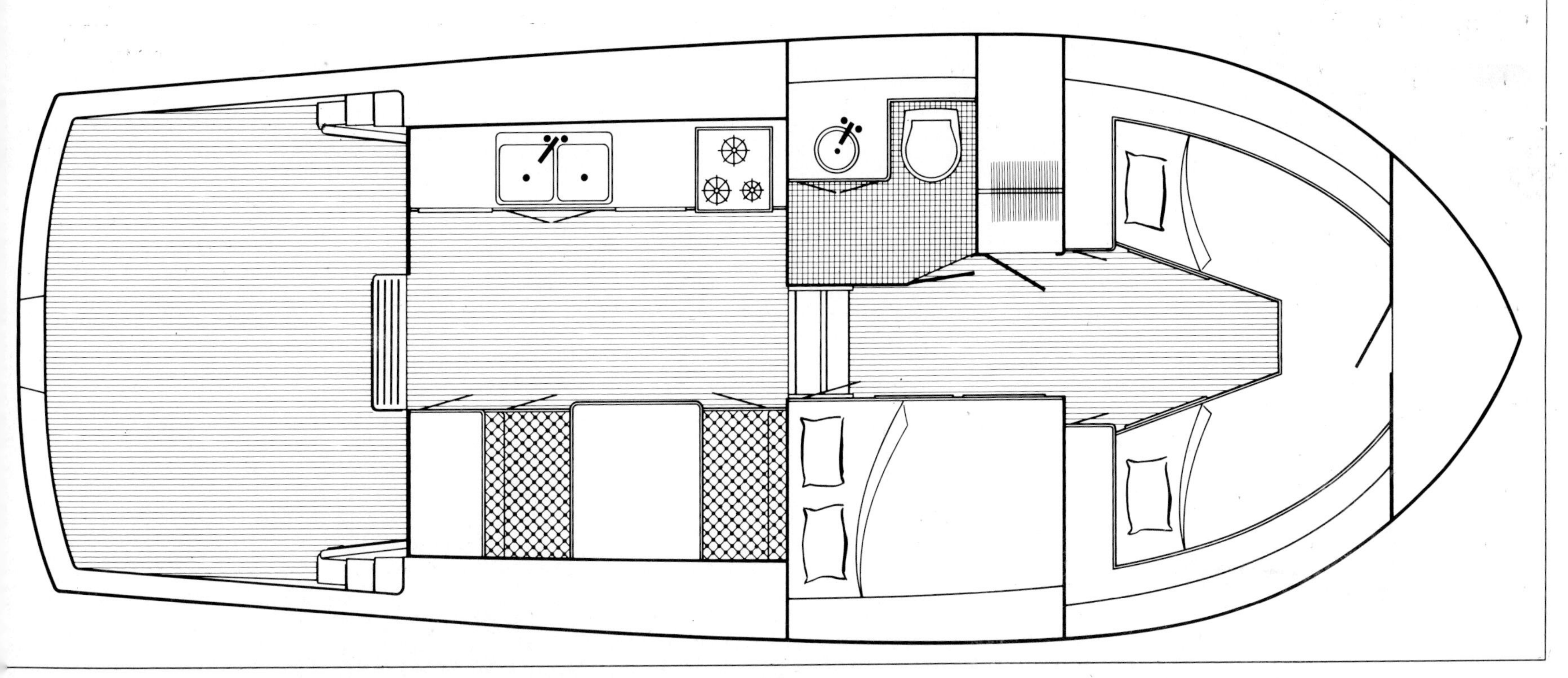

All of the Grand Banks cruising power yachts were designed by my friend Kenneth L. Smith, formerly of Fairfield, Connecticut and now retired to New Gloucester, Maine. Ken and I first met many years ago at Joel Johnson's boat shop in Black Rock, Connecticut, and we have maintained a close friendship ever since. In passing, Ken is one of the most generous and helpful fellows anyone could know, and we shared many grand experiences over the years. He was also a first-class, practical yacht designer in addition to being president of the J. L. Lucas Machine Company, of Bridgeport, a firm which specializes in rebuilding heavy machinery for industry. Ken designed the Boothbay 33-footers and a good many other proven power yachts, but surely the most famous of all his designs are the Grand Banks diesel cruisers.

The Grand Banks boats were originally built of teak and other Oriental wood by the Newton family in Hong Kong. The interesting history of the development of the boats and the tribulations of the Hong Kong firm appears in Nautical Quarterly 4 and is a fascinating history of Grand Banks in its first 15 years.

Rick Loh, associated with his father Dick, told me at our meeting in Essex, Connecticut, when I inspected a new 42-footer, that Ken had designed the first Grand Banks in about 1963, and that they were built of wood until the fall of 1973. The firm, based now in Singapore, produces the single-screw Grand Banks 32, which is my favorite, in addition to the 36, the 42 and the 49. The 42′ "Standard" is the most popular Grand Banks boat, and some 700 have been built, about half at the original Grand Banks plant in Hong Kong, the remainder built in Singapore by American Marine (S) PTE Ltd. of fiberglass-reinforced plastic since 1973. The 42-footer is also offered under the name "Europa" in "Sportcruiser" and "Motor Yacht" versions. The "Standard" is by far the best accepted.

I inspected Grand Banks 42 hull No. 738, and I must say I found that, while nothing is perfect, being critical of near perfection is a difficult task. In acquiring a Grand Banks trawler yacht you come pretty darned close to obtaining perfection. I will digress here a moment to discuss perfectionism and the art of being hypercritical—in very personal terms. The late yacht designer Frederick K. Lord, an old shipmate of mine and my father's, was a perfectionist. That dear man was one of the most critical people I have ever run across. Nothing completely pleased him. It was my practice in years past, before Fred slid off to Valhalla, to drive him to his annual class reunion at the New York State Military Academy at Peekskill, New York, and it *was* a tiresome day. From starting off at New Rochelle rather early in the morning and returning late at night, Fred would continually criticize, question and ponder all manner of things. "God damn it, John," he would say, "why do they always make bridge railings just the wrong height to prevent you from seeing the river?" Or, in passing a gasoline station with hundreds of plastic pennants flying to attract attention, Fred would say, "God damn it, John, they could use half as many flags and it would be

GRAND BANKS 42 A SURVEY BY JOHN ATKIN

just as effective." Another of his questions related to a cricket that lived in the elevator in his apartment at New Rochelle. Fred would say, "God damn it, John, what do you suppose that cricket eats? There is nothing in there but grease." Another of Fred's observations might be: "The Lord made some—let's say 500,000—of various species of insects. God damn it, John, why don't you suppose he didn't just make a hundred, or two hundred? That would have been plenty."

I have a strong notion that even Frederick K. Lord would have had some difficulty in finding anything to criticize on the Grand Banks 42. As I observed the boat's details, which were a fetish with Fred, I could not help but recall him and feel that he would have been favorably impressed by the attention to detail I was seeing. Dear Fred Lord—his memory will always be with me.

I have always felt that the Grand Banks hulls are particularly well conceived. The proportions between beam and length in all of these boats approaches the ideal. I ponder the amount of flare and flam that Ken Smith introduced in the 42's topsides forward. This is a difficult area to evaluate, and while many of the various "trawlers" built in the Far East, in my observation, have excessively strong flare and flam which I feel may give them a tendency to "stop themselves" in any kind of a head sea; on the other hand they may be a bit drier than the Grand Banks. I must say, a bit more flare forward on Grand Banks boats would appeal to me, although not to the degree of some of the very excessive flare I've observed. Just another area of compromise. The hulls are conventional "warped-plane," V-bottom boats—very much after the manner of many wholesome V-bottoms designed over many years. There is nothing original about the hull form. It is traditional, and I'll use the term old-fashioned V-bottom boat to describe this hull form which has gained great popularity through intelligent marketing by American Marine as well as through the experience of Ken Smith and a great many satisfied owners. In saying "old-fashioned" I am not being critical. I mean old-fashioned in the most constructive sense, because I feel there is a lot to be learned from past experience. In talking to various owners of these boats over the years, I have been told and have observed myself, that the Grand Banks isn't essentially the finest sea boat that was ever conceived. However, in one way or another it has managed to gain that reputation. I

John Atkin remarks that the GB42's engine compartment is neat enough and roomy enough for the skipper and his guests to sit down for cocktails in this 4'6"-high space and enjoy themselves admiring the installation of the two Lehman/Ford diesels, Onan generating plant, tanks, pipes and clean looms of wiring.

The Grand Banks 42 is an especially well-conceived little ship, from her workboat-inspired lines down to the smallest details of her equipment and construction. The arrangement plan below shows the standard model with its bright, roomy saloon and fore and aft staterooms. There are two other models

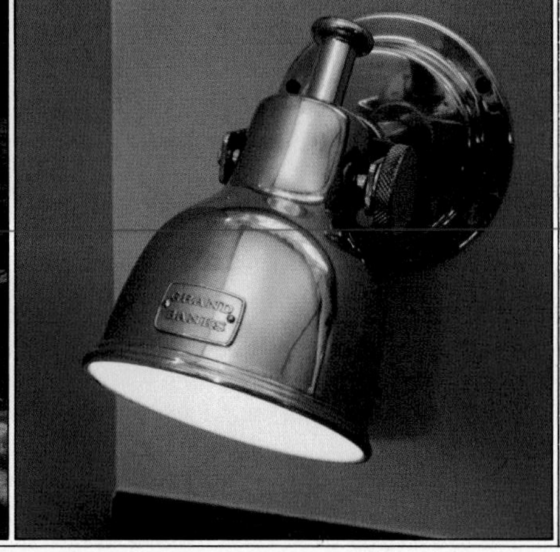

of the GB42—a Sports Cruiser with a 12′ x 9′ teak cockpit aft, and a similar Europa model with an extended hardtop over the cockpit.

LOA: 42′7″
Beam: 13′8″
Draft: 4′2½″
Displacement: 34,000 pounds
Hull: Hand-layup fiberglass
Power: Twin 120-hp Lehman/Ford diesels
Fuel: 600 gallons
Water: 316 gallons
Designer: Kenneth L. Smith
Builder: American Marine (S) PTE Ltd. of Singapore
U.S. Address: Grand Banks Yachts Ltd., 270 Greenwich Ave., Greenwich, CT 06830

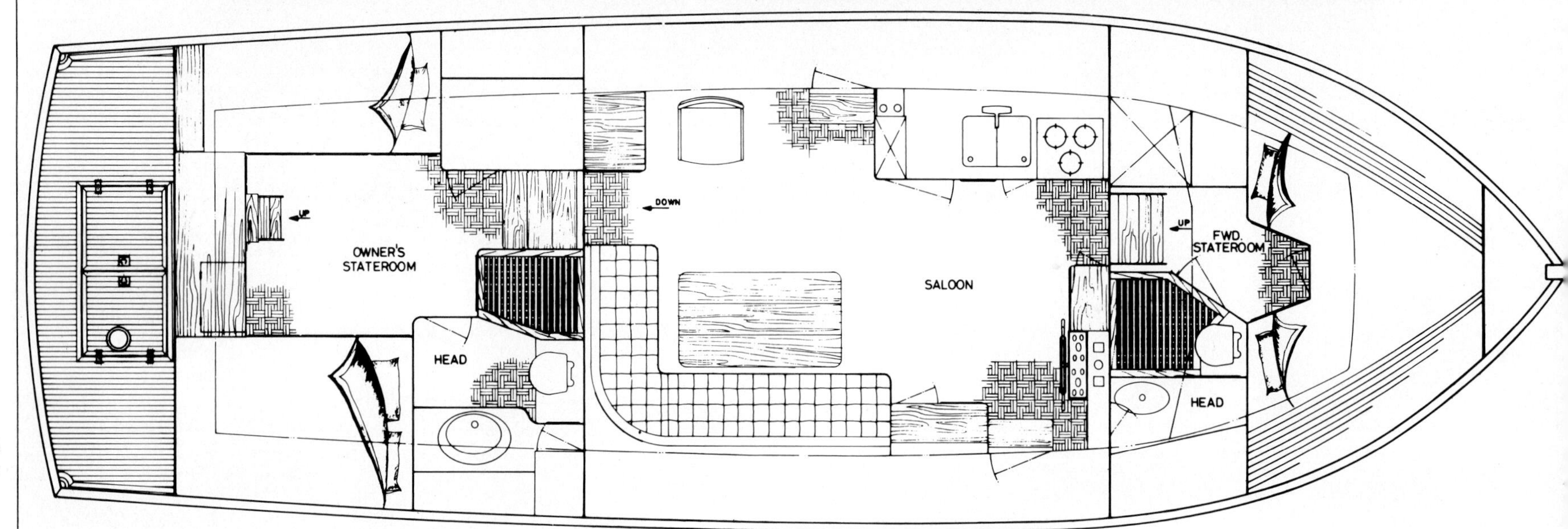

suspect that much of this is related to the wholesome appearance of Grand Banks boats. Perhaps I should say here that all boats will do their share of rolling in a beam sea or when conditions—weather, wind and waves–are bad. This is one reason why Ken Smith arranged for the small steadying sail to be set on a mast and boom at the after end of the 42's deckhouse—to dampen her motion. On the 42-footer, by the way, these spars are aluminum and handsomely painted white.

In getting involved with Grand Banks hull No. 738, I found the quality of the workmanship to be superb—absolutely superb! The details of the rail endings, for example, with their turnbacks bow and stern, are simply a handsome piece of work. The teak rails are supported by bronze stanchions which in turn are screw-fastened to the rail caps through heavy bronze pads. All very rigidly fastened and all very strong. The degree of finish of the varnish and the quality of workmanship of the locked scarf joinings in her rails—in fact, the workmanship overall—is perfectly executed.

At the bow end of the yacht there is an anchor-handling pulpit arranged to accommodate a CQR or a Danforth anchor over two rollers, one at the forward end of the pulpit and one at its after end. The shank of the anchor travels over the forward roller, and the chain, in turn, follows over the after roller and down to a deck pipe into the ground-tackle locker. An electric-or manual-anchor windlass can be installed in accordance with the owner's wishes.

Grand Banks boats are entirely fiberglass-reinforced plastic. There is no plywood encased or covered in any manner. The main decks are fiberglass with teak laid over them. It is my understanding that these teak decks are machine-screw fastened, tapped into the glass laminate and obviously bunged over. The synthetic material in the deck seams is applied in a professional manner, and, as might be hoped, there is no indication of adhesion failure on this new yacht. The half-round moldings and handrails are first-quality teak. I am not qualified to identify Burma teak from other Oriental teaks, but the wood on these boats is obviously well-seasoned and far superior to other "teaks" I have had the opportunity to observe on numerous Far East yachts.

One thing I noticed on deck is a complete lack of freeing ports in, or under, the bulwark rail. Water on the 42's decks has to run aft to her quarters where there are scuppers of large diameter. To be sure, this arrangement eliminates the streaking commonly found where there are openings under the rail, but it does have a tendency, in anything of a sea condition, to have any water taken aboard travel from bow to stern before it is eliminated. No big problem, to be sure, but it is a "detail" that Fred Lord might have found disturbing. There is a plastic hinge on the upper edge of the bridge deck windshield opening on her centerline. I have observed the tendency of these to fatigue reasonably early in the game, and it is a bit of a mystery why the Grand Banks firm would incorporate them in lieu of a proven chrome-plated brass piano hinge. Accountants who oversee the costs of building boats often create problems that the owner has to cope with.

In a further critical vein, one nice feature would be a teak covering board, or plank sheer, at the outboard edge of the decks. Earlier Grand Banks yachts incorporated this nicety. But in the interest of economics it is evident the accountants dictated that planks which simply joggle at their outboard ends are satisfactory even though they lack the professional appearance of earlier models or of a Consolidated- or a Luders-built yacht. This is another detail—but it is details that create perfection.

Ken Smith arranged the sliding windows and glass channels outboard the house sides. His purpose in doing this was to eliminate the prospect of rainwater or seawater gaining access into the deckhouse sides. This concept has been maintained, and it is a practical arrangement with the after end of the window trim and gutter provided with an ample scupper to free any water accumulation outside of the house or trunk cabin. One thing the owner wants to do, in the interest of maintenance, is to be certain the scuppers at the cabin windows are kept clean and free to flow. Over the years, in past surveys of used Grand Banks, I have found the window frames to be subject to deterioration at their lower corners, in way of the scuppers, and they certainly want to be well-maintained.

There is an altogether shipshape atmosphere aboard a Grand Banks yacht like this one. She reflects the background of Ken Smith, and she reflects the background of Dick Loh and his able associates who are involved in the yacht's building. The lack of "wall-to-wall" shag carpeting is refreshing! The parquet cabin soles, instead, are handsome indeed. There is teak laid on the fiberglass trunk cabin aft to provide anti-skid properties as you gain access to the bridge deck overhead. On the upper bridge there is an efficient wind deflector extending athwartships made of plexiglas much after those on the Grand Banks of years gone by. Standard instrumentation on the new Grand Banks 42 consists of tachometers for the two engines, ammeters, water temperature and oil pressure gauges, Morse engine controls, and reverse gear and throttle to either hand. The steering wheel is of teak and beautifully made and finished. Steering is accomplished by flexible stainless-steel wire running over large-diameter, hard-plastic sheaves to a bronze quadrant. This works like a charm and has the advantage of being practical, simple and dependable. There are strong stops which the rudder quadrant fetches up against when the wheel is hard over. I have seen installations where no stops are installed, and this exerts considerable stress on the steering cable and its components and is, naturally, undesirable. The wheel turns 2-1/4 times to obtain hard over to hard over. There is a Danforth "Constellation" compass mounted directly forward of the wheel. There is an exhaust blower arranged over the galley stove which is tucked to port outboard the bridge wing.

The quality of the 'glass work on these boats is absolutely first-class. There are no loose ends, ragged ends of 'glass cloth or evidence of L. Francis Herreshoff's "frozen snot" oozing out of various joinings, nor any indication of slipshod workmanship. I feel the quality is impressively high. The wiring at Hull No. 738's flying bridge wing to starboard, as well as the balance of her wiring installation, is extremely well organized, neatly loomed and reflects the best workmanship.

The quality of the 'glass work on these boats is absolutely first-class. There are no loose ends or any indication of slipshod workmanship.

Her West Coast transom platform is professionally made and finished. Its corners are protected by half-oval bronze straps let into the edge of the teak. There is a varnished teak overlay on the transom. While I am not particularly enamored of this wood treatment, which incorporates prominent V grooves between the strakes, that is purely a matter of taste. If this were my Grand Banks 42, I would like to see her transom of white fiberglass laminate with a glossy gelcoat finish, which is an option. I feel the V joints appear to be "busy" and that smooth planking would, to my mind, be far more attractive. Rick Loh told me that they had experienced varied opinions on the treatment of the transom.

The hull and sheer guard are protected by half-oval bronze molding to protect these against chafing. The docking lines are arranged in a traditional manner with bow chocks either hand as well as in her bulwark rail for spring lines amidship and stern lines at her quarters. I am often a bit astounded, in surveying contemporary production yachts, to find no bow chocks in many instances; the anchor rode and dock lines are simply made up to inadequate cleats to port and starboard just abaft the stem head.

There is a Dyer FRP dinghy secured in proper chocks on the after trunk cabin overhead. This is arranged to be launched by using the boom of the steadying rig. Many owners install an electric winch on the mast to ease the work of launching and hauling the dink.

Stainless-steel water tanks are well chocked directly forward of the transom in the lazarette, and these are equipped with plastic "sight gauges" on their forward sides. The fills are at the tanks directly below the cockpit hatches. Inspection of the fiberglass layup in the lazarette again reflects a very high standard of workmanship.

It is evident that the sheer guard is molded into the topsides. The bulwark rail, in turn, is incorporated in the deck mold. The bulwark is hollow and the docking cleats are bolted to the inboard face of the rail. Thus there is no means, as there is no access, to the fastenings of these in the event that one should be torn free. It would be, if you will excuse the expression, something of a "Chinese puzzle" to determine just how to go about refastening the cleat. When I pointed this out to Dick and Rick Loh, they acknowledged it could present a problem. But Dick explained that there is a very heavy metal doubling plate through which the cleat's bolts run, with nuts outboard of the doubler. He also said they had never experienced one of the cleats being torn free. However, I can envision the installation being a concern in the event a tremendous strain were exerted on one of the cleats. Its proper repair would be a complex and expensive undertaking.

The Grand Banks 42 engine compartment is a grand piece of engineering in all respects. With some 4′6″ of headroom it would be quite possible for the skipper and his guests to enjoy cocktails in the engine-room, and for those mechanically inclined I am sure there would be many favorable comments on the fine accessibility of the various components. It is possible to sit comfortably outboard either of the two Lehman/Ford diesel engines. These are freshwater-cooled engines built by the Ford Motor Company to power trucks and industrial equipment, and they are converted for marine use by Lehman at Linden, New Jersey. Each 380-cu.-in. engine develops 120 hp at 2500 rpm. These Lehman/Ford engines have enjoyed a fine reputation for dependability for a good many years. Like all good engineering they are basically simple. The two engines consume a total of about 4 gallons an hour turning 1600 rpm, and the yacht's speed is 8.5 knots. Turning 2000 rpm, her speed is 10 knots and uses 5.5 gallons of fuel per hour. It is evident that these diesels are not only dependable but also very efficient. The engines are provided with full-way seacocks, as are all through-hull penetrations, in addition to sea strainers on the raw-water intakes.

An Onan generating plant is installed on the hull centerline just abaft the main engines. This is equipped with a sound shield and one of Onan's Aqua-hush mufflers, and it creates surprisingly little fuss when running with the engine hatches closed.

Steel fuel tanks are well installed to port and starboard outboard the main engines. Naturally, these fill from deck, are vented outboard and equipped with fuel return lines. They are also fitted with clear plastic "sight" tubes on their inboard faces. In the past I have come across similar installations on Grand Banks boats I have surveyed to find that the sight tubes had been removed and the spuds that feed them plugged. Referring to current National Fire Protection Association standard No. 302 I found, under the fuel system section, specifically 5-4.8, that "the use of gauge glasses shall be restricted to day or service tanks of diesel-fuel systems." I have a great deal of respect for the N.F.P.A. standards, as do many leading insurance underwriters. I would, therefore, if I were involved with the Grand Banks yachts, install fuel gauges at the helm and eliminate the prospect of a bilge full of fuel oil in the event that one of the fittings on the sight tubes happened to fail.

Additional equipment in the engine compartment includes a 12-gallon Raritan hot water heater, a Sentry battery charger, Jabsco macerator pump and fiberglass effluent holding tank conforming to current E.P.A. regulations. The main engine hangers, by the way, land on heavy aluminum angle which caps ample fore and aft stringers firmly glassed to the yacht's underbody.

I am impressed by what I consider to be the great simplicity of the boat's machinery installation. It is all most accessible, and there is no reason that the compartment should ever get dirty or messy with normal maintenance. It is, again, typically Grand Banks engineering, a thing that bespeaks knowledgeable people producing these yachts.

I have had the opportunity, in the past, to run a sister ship of this 42 from Stamford down to City Island, and I've been aboard a good many other Grand Banks. It is evident that they are efficiently driven hulls. Rich Loh calls them semi-displacement hulls, but I find this is difficult terminology to come to terms with. The FRP hulls are ballasted with a mixture of copper slag and resin in the hollow keel. Because of the hull form and the ballast I feel they are true displacement hulls. However, my opinion is confounded by a chap down in Florida, whom Rick told me about, who installed turbocharged diesels, trim tabs at her transom, and otherwise went about achieving a speed of 21 mph with one of the 42-footers. On *that* basis she is a semi-planing hull. But I feel strongly that Ken's concept was to produce a displacement hull, or a semi-displacement hull, and that this applies to the majority of the Grand Banks.

I am aware that my old friend Fred Lord never heard of Bo Derek. It was after his time that a scoring system from one to ten was established for the recognition of certain physical attributes. I would certainly have to rate the Grand Banks a very high nine or a low ten on the Bo Derek scale, and I have a notion that Fred Lord would concur.

Aug. 19, 1981. 0530, 3rd day out. C—095. S—5K. W—SW 10K.

With usual forehandedness, started working on my Christmas list. Remembered that my crew gave me NAUTICAL QUARTERLY last year. Terrific present! Why not give a subscription this year to my navigator, my spinnaker man, the yacht club manager, my one-design sailor son, my broker who's just been bitten by the sea bug? What better way to tell them all year 'round just how much I appreciate them?

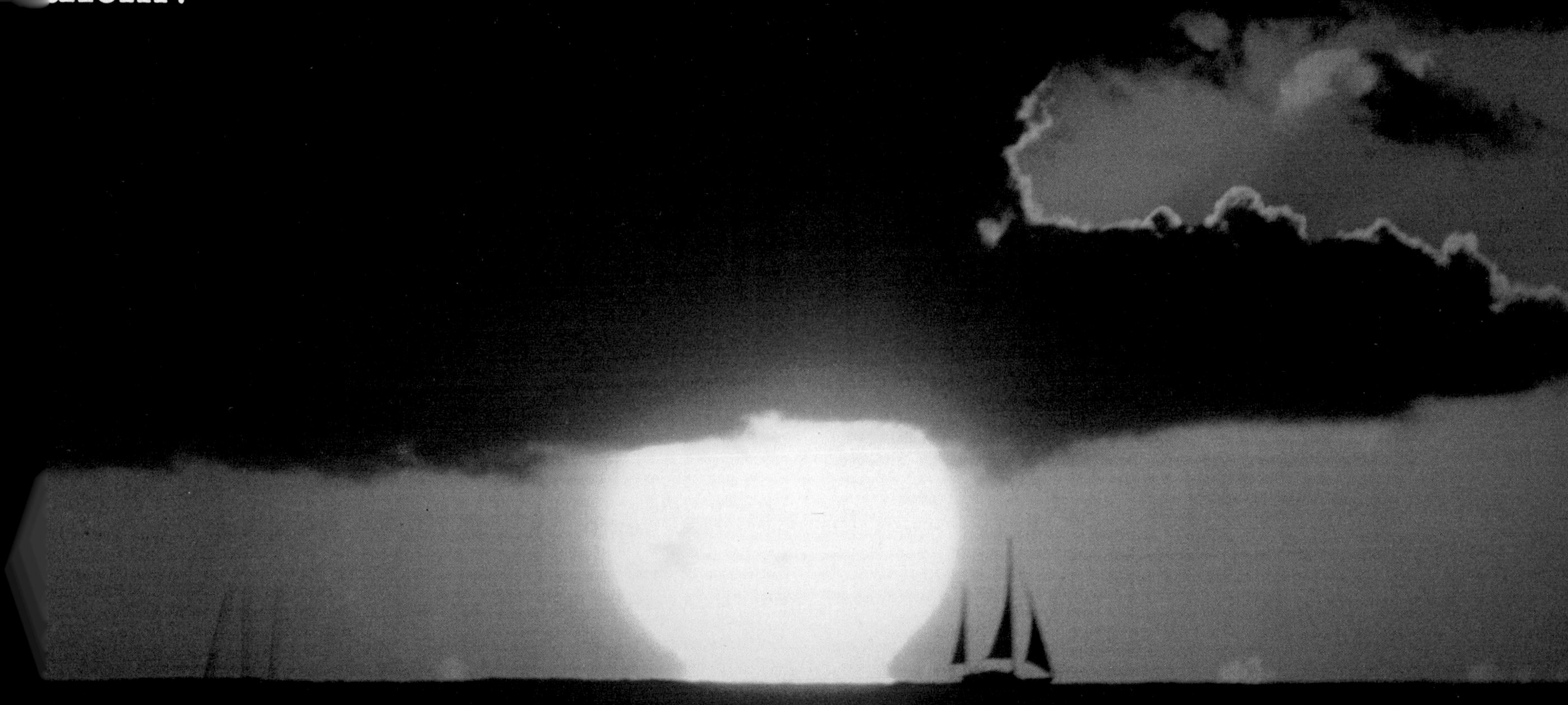

DON'T FORGET AND DON'T BE FORGOTTEN. **TAKE ADVANTAGE OF OUR SPECIAL SEASONAL RATES** **AND SAVE UP TO $7.00 ON EACH GIFT SUBSCRIPTION.** **ORDER TODAY!**

NAUTICAL QUARTERLY is normally $49.50 per year by subscription, but your first gift (or your own renewal) is only $45.00, and additional gifts are only $42.50. We'll send a handsome, hand-inscribed gift card with your personal message to all those on your holiday gift list. If the attached order card is missing, send your instructions to: Gift Order Desk, NAUTICAL QUARTERLY Subscription Services, Depot Square, Peterborough, NH 03458. Special rates expire 1/15/82.

COMPLETE YOUR COLLECTION NOW.

A limited number of back issues of NAUTICAL QUARTERLY are still available at the special price of $12.50 each (non-subscribers please send $15.00) postpaid. Please send check or bank card information to:

Back Issues
NAUTICAL QUARTERLY
373 Park Avenue South
New York, NY 10016

Use the order envelope in front of this issue for fastest service.

NQ1

The schooner *America's* 1851 triumph; Sir Thomas Lipton's five attempts to seize the Ould Mug; The great J Boats of the 1930s; Twelve-meter technology, from *Vim* to *Sverige;* Detailed profiles of 1977 Cup contenders; A social history of America's Cup spectating; An America's Cup chronology—1851 to 1974; 35 Cup contenders in dramatic paintings and photos; Bus Mosbacher on training, tuning and sailing to win;

NQ2

Dick Newick and his trans-Atlantic trimarans; Ten crazy, creative years of offshore powerboat racing; Baron Marcel Bich's breathtaking *Shenandoah*; The Roaring Forties and the Howling Fifties; The yacht-design artistry of C.G. Davis; Profiles of six special boats; Tahiti—that legendary landfall; The story of the U.S. Coast Pilot;

NQ3

The SORC—ocean racing's World Series; The Great Whales, their lives, their survival; Coldmolding—boatbuilding's new/old way with wood; The roaring years of rumrunning; Profiles of four exceptional boats; Joshua Slocum's career as a shipmaster; April on the Alaskan salmon grounds;

NQ4

The extraordinary Italian style in boats; Two men who rowed transAtlantic in a 16′ skiff; A William Garden pirate-ship/yacht; The new rowing boats probed and photographed; Nature's bounty on three U.S. coasts; Westsail and Grand Banks—an enlightening look at success and failure in the boatbuilding game; The luminous marine art of Carl G. Evers; Profiles of four outstanding production boats; A revealing portrait of Olin Stephens;

NQ5

Friendship sloops; The life and times of the seagull; Aboard a Thames barge trading foreign in the late 'thirties; Analyzing the live-aboard lifestyle; A natural history of the lobsterboat; The revival of commercial sail; Three semi-custom boats and the wild C-Class Catamaran profiled; The products and politics of the liferaft industry; An inquiry into the fuel efficiency of powerboats;

NQ6

Rocky Aoki on the offshore powerboat circuit; Russell Hoyt on the offshore sailing circuit; A replica clipper ship proposed for New York and the world; Louise Burke, *Mistral* and the Naval Academy's sailing program; Teaching boatbuilding and pure resourcefulness at Maine's Apprenticeshop; Sterling Hayden recounts the last of the Fisherman's Cup Races; John Atkin surveys six current production boats;

NQ7

A hundred years of Chris-Craft history; The daring decades of last-century sandbagger racing; The philosophy and psychology of singlehanding; Living aboard—a rare, rewarding lifestyle; Hermann Goering's extraordinary Dutch botter-jacht; Bob Perry and cruising yachts designed for speed; Haunting photographs from the New England of your grandfather's day; Four new and special production boats; Captain Kittredge's affordable sport submarine; David Lewis discusses the Stone-Age navigation of the South Seas;

NQ8

The extraordinary boats of Henry R. Hinckley & Co., including closeups of the Bermuda 40, Sou'wester 50 and Hinckley 64; The boats and men of the East Coast dope trade; Aboard a tugboat/home in Sausalito; Richard Ellis portrays the world's dolphins in words and lovely paintings; Jim Wynne's career as one of the world's eminent powerboat designers; An appreciation of Alf Loomis by John Rousmaniere; Fiberglass boat-building, from the disasters of the 1940s to the Kevlar laminates of the moment; John Atkin surveys and compares the Hinckley Bermuda 40 and the Gulfstar 40;

NQ9

Mike Levitt reports on the 1979 Admiral's Cup spectacle and the tragic Fastnet Race; Fifty-plus years of ocean-racing glory aboard the schooner *Niña;* The New England dory defined, discussed, admired and exemplified by six contemporary boats photographed in color by Allan Weitz; An appreciation of L. Francis Herreshoff by Phil Bolger; Extraordinary Sam Abell photographs of the island of Newfoundland; Living and working aboard a 'thirties motor yacht; Joe Upton's dramatic log of a winter in the Alaska king crab fishery;

NQ10

Twenty years of the Observer Singlehanded Translantic Race, including accounts and color photos of 1980's contenders; A revealing portrait of Bernie Goldhirsh, the phenomenon behind the phenomenon of Sail magazine; A bone-chilling view of the Ghosts of Cape Horn with haunting 100-year-old-photographs; A scrutable examination of heretofore inscrutable Chinese boatbuilding in teak and fiberglass; The story of *Lord Jim,* San Francisco's superbly restored Alden schooner; Visionary powerboats for the 1980s from Marine and Aero Design;

NQ11

Shahbaz, a 50-knot diesel cruiser from Sardinia; Brendan Gill's lively and lovely appreciation of summer on Canada's Muskoka lakes, accompanied by Dudley Witney's rich photography; a profile of Ernest Gann—writer, sailor, aviator, marine painter; The history of the catboat, from 1850 to 1980, including four appealing examples photographed in color; Mike Levitt's review of the seven contenders for the America's Cup in 1980; A million-dollar aluminum sportfisherman from New Orleans; the high-tech Stiletto, a multihull for the eighties; John Rousmaniere's fascinating analysis of America's Cup defense campaigns from 1870 to 1980;

NQ12

The Vikings and their extraordinary ships, with stunning photographs by Ted Spiegel; Nim Marsh explores the heritage and handiness of a boat designed by a fish—the New England bass boat; Eight items of great gear reviewed by Peter Spectre; Yacht racing in miniature; Ron Holland—a portrait of the artist as a young man; Four good boats reviewed, three with color photographs, including Ron Holland's new *Infinity;* A visit aboard a nautical guest house; The fascinating behavior of the Gulf Stream explained by meteorologist Colleen Leary;

NQ13

Richard Ellis tells us what we know and what we only think we know about sharks; Don Aronow, the racing and boatbuilding phenomenon behind Cigarette and Squadron XII sport powerboats; The story of World War II's "Hooligan Navy"; Visits aboard six extraordinary barges in Paris; The Ocean Cruising 40 surveyed by John Atkin; An excerpt from Rockwell Kent's classic *N by E,* and an update on the equally classic cutter *Direction;* Reviews of three outstanding new boats; The story of Palmer Johnson, a Wisconsin boatyard where world-class yachts are built;

NQ14

John Hacker and 60 years of designing great American powerboats; The Waterway, that North-South path through water and time; Jim Kilroy and the development of the new *Kialoa;* visiting a family of three aboard their 20′ home—a Flicka sloop; the saga of *Sea Cloud,* Marjorie Merriweather Post's square-rigged yacht, now a Bristol-fashion charter vessel; L. Francis Herreshoff's sail in his father's *Alerion,* with photos of the new *Alerion* replica; the lives and easy times of yachting's professional hands; three exceptional boats reviewed, including Phil Bolger's 31′ Folding Schooner.

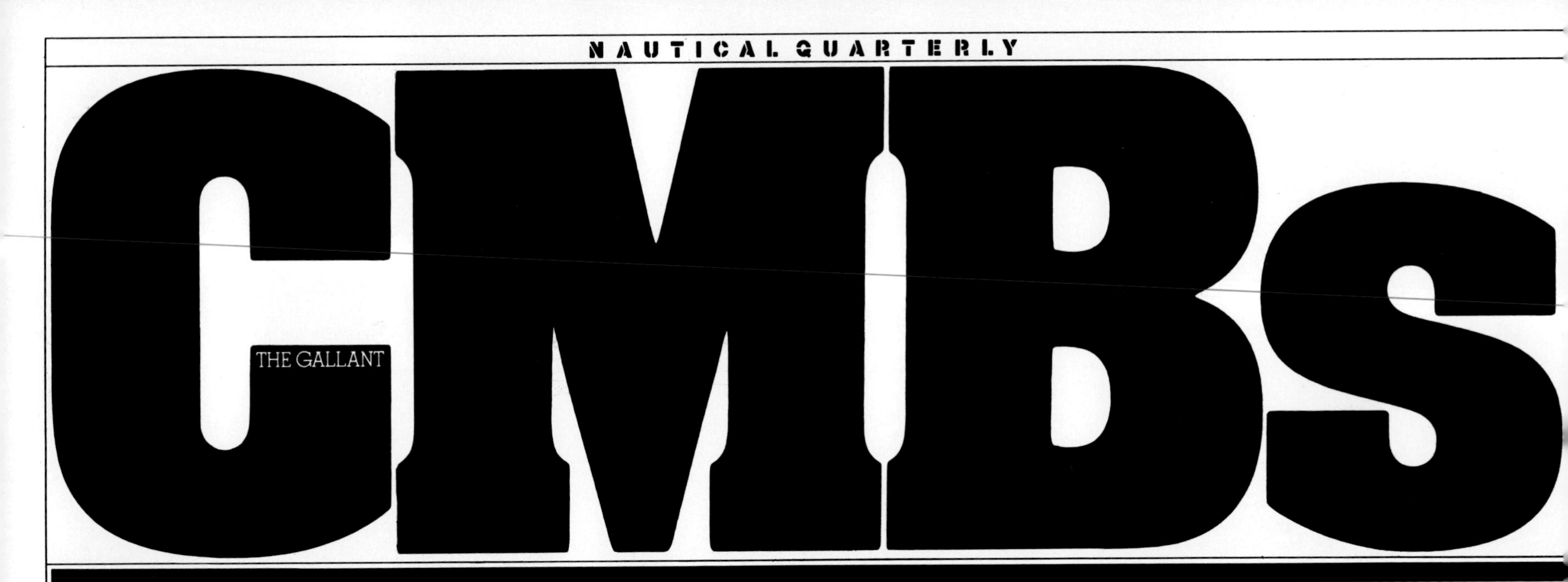

The British Admiralty dubbed them CMBs, an unromantic name which suggested nothing of their substance, although "dubbed," with its echo of knighthood, is perhaps the appropriate verb to use here. In their role of roving wielders of torpedoes, the CMBs were knights errant, slayers of dragons, gallant vehicles with skilled, single-minded and courageous men aboard. □ The British Coastal Motor Boats of World War I were the smallest and fastest naval vessels of their time. Armed with torpedoes, they could attack and sink ships hundreds of times their size, and their depth charges were the scourge of the enemy's new submarines. The low profiles and sleek lines of these boats were a matter of function, and the young men aboard them were every bit the counterpart of their much-publicized comrades in the Spads and Nieuports of the aerial war.

BY DANIEL L. WILKINS

T

After a year of war, the lack of high-seas battles, and the rapid onset of small coastal engagements in European waters, soon resurrected the idea of the small high-speed torpedo boat.

The brief history of these boats begins with that fearsome weapon of modern naval warfare—the torpedo. Because of the large load of explosive carried and the damping effect of water, which concentrated the explosion in one direction, the Whitehead torpedo, developed in 1872, had greater destructive power than any naval weapon that had come before it. Because of the short range and slow speed of the torpedo and because of the great defensive strength of its intended targets, success by torpedo boats could be expected only through surprise attack at close quarters under the cover of darkness. In the 1870s, small boats of high speed were seen as the right type of vessel to fight with the torpedo. But during the 40 years preceding W.W.I, torpedo boats grew in size until they were really small cruisers. The high speeds of these steam-powered little ships (35 knots) eclipsed the usefulness of the original small torpedo boats, which then could use only heavy internal-combustion engines for power. These larger boats, in fact, soon became known as Torpedo Boat Destroyers, later shortened to destroyers.

The early fighting of World War I showed that the work of these destroyers would be done primarily by their guns. At the same time, the very extensive use of mines by the Germans made it hazardous for submarines and vessels of any considerable draft to approach enemy bases. By mid-1915, the small high-speed boat became again the obvious means of carrying the Whitehead torpedo to the enemy.

Broadly speaking, Britain's plan of naval campaign at the outbreak of World War I aimed, first, to destroy the German and Austrian fleets with superior forces or, failing this, to confine the enemy and restrict his trade by a system of distant blockades, and, second, to destroy, capture, or bottle-up enemy warships operating on foreign stations. The weaker German and Austrian navies envisioned a different kind of campaign. They planned, first, to operate the home fleets as protection for their coastlines and to control as much of the sea beyond as possible to prevent a close blockade; second, they hoped to use their naval vessels abroad to inflict maximum damage on the enemy before escaping to the shelter of home or friendly ports. They intended to damage the enemy by interfering with commerce in submarines and by fighting attrition warfare—harassing and menacing the superior allied navies by instituting fast air and sea raids, attacking with torpedoes, and making extensive use of mines.

In the years before 1914, rapid advances in small planing-boat design were being made in racing, using ever-lighter and faster engines developed for the new automobiles. The Championship of the Seas in Monaco, the Prix de Nations, and the Harmsworth Cup spurred innovation in planing-hull technology by leaps. *Maple Leaf IV,* a multiple-step hydroplane, became the first boat to reach a speed of 50 knots in winning the 1912-13 races for the Harmsworth Trophy, as one eminent example. At the same time, development of larger and lighter gasoline engines, particularly for aircraft, continued. After a year of war, the lack of high-seas battles and the rapid onset of small coastal engagements in European waters, soon resurrected the idea of the small high-speed torpedo boat.

In early 1915, Sublieutenants Hampden, Bremner, and Anson of the Harwich Striking Force, disappointed at the way in which developments were restricting the activities of the British High Seas Fleet, suggested the building of small, fast motorboats to be carried aboard cruisers in davits. These would be transported to the minefields in the German Bight and, with their light draft, would safely pass over the mines to launch torpedo attacks on the German High Seas Fleet. This was a return to the idea of small torpedo boats operating from larger vessels, but it was modified to deal with the special needs that arose from the progress of the war. Success could only be expected if the boats were so small, fast, and maneuverable that from the time of being sighted until the moment of firing the torpedo, the enemy would be unable to take evasive action. As well as minimum size and adequate range, a speed of at least 30 knots with torpedo aboard was considered essential. The pioneer of British torpedo-boat building John I. Thornycroft & Co. Ltd. had been developing a boat along these lines and so took up the three naval officers' promising idea as a private venture.

Although the prevalent pre-war flatbottom boats with rectangular sections planed well, they slammed violently even in slightly rough water. Thornycrofts decided on a stepped hull with a slightly warped run aft of the step to improve seaworthiness. The normal fine lines forward were retained, with a sharp angle of chine rising from step to stem as necessitated by the lifting bow, a thing that also improved directional stability and damped down the bow wave. The torpedo-discharge gear presented some problems. From the very beginning it was clear that a normal torpedo tube (compressed-air or explosive ejection) was not possible due to weight alone, and that it was essential to incorporate the torpedo layout within the framework of the boat. From a tactical viewpoint the torpedo had to be fired while the boat was moving at top speed if success was to be achieved. The obvious arrangement of fitting the torpedo forward, as in the slower torpedo boats of the 19th century, was rejected on ballistic and hydrodynamic grounds. The alternative was a stern layout, which would be better for a hydroplane. But the boat would have to turn away stern-to before firing, and this would reduce the chances of success and increase the possibility of the boat being hit by opposing fire. Then quite a new idea was proposed: if the boat's speed were over 30 knots, about full torpedo speed, the torpedo could be stowed head forward on rails and launched tail first over the stern, where it would start up automatically. The stern needed only to be given a trough in which the

The greatest secrecy was maintained throughout the design, building, and training operations of the CMBs, as their success would depend very much on the enemy's ignorance of their existence.

torpedo could slide on rails, and the sides of the trough would serve as longitudinal girders aft. These girders would extend forward and also serve as engine bearers and forward longitudinals, thus increasing the strength of the entire hull. Side plates at the stern would steady the torpedo until it was clear of the boat.

The minimum speed for successful torpedo launching was about 18 knots. The torpedo was aimed by lining the boat up on target and, as soon as the torpedo was launched, swerving the boat sharply away out of the torpedo's track. To prevent icing up in winter, the engine exhaust could be directed to warm the rails. The advantages of the layout were its simplicity and economy of weight, the position of the very heavy torpedo in the most favorable part of the boat, and the ability to launch the torpedo even at top speed. The disadvantages were the lack of protection for the torpedo and the danger of not swerving away in time if a torpedo failed or ran along the surface.

The boat was a minor marvel. A 40′, 8.5′-beam, 9500-pound displacement prototype was built entirely of American elm. The construction was ingenious, with closely spaced continuous-bent transverse frames and longitudinals, and with a double-diagonal laminated skin. To this very strong monocoque structure was added a false bottom which gave the desired hull form, step, and hard chines. The boat was a single-step hydroplane with a rounded forepart, double frames amidships, continuous longitudinal girders, and relatively flat sections aft. At an operational displacement of 9570 pounds, and with a 250-hp engine driving a 19″-diameter propeller, she made 33.5 knots on trials in the spring of 1916. An alternative spiral propeller, used to prevent entanglement with netting and barricades, was also tested and the loss of speed was only .75 knots. Carrying 125 gallons of gasoline, the little boat's range at speed was 160 nautical miles.

The performance of the prototype, CMB-1, caused the Admiralty to accept her and order another twelve boats to be delivered in 1916. As the Admiralty decided to build a large number of CMBs with all speed, arrangements were made with other firms accustomed to light boatbuilding to build to Thornycroft designs. So many boatbuilders had left their ordinary work to go to the airplane factories that it was difficult to find men with the right skills, and many boats were built by men with no previous boatbuilding experience. As no suitable engines existed for the prototype, new designs were prepared, and the motors were built at the Thornycroft Basingstoke Works, where the torpedo gear and fittings were also made. Subsequent motors were built there or adapted from airplane engines such as Greens, Fiats, and Sunbeams. With only a few exceptions, the CMBs deliberately ran without silencers in order to simulate airplanes and mislead the enemy.

In 1917 a bigger 55′ CMB prototype was built and equipped with two stern torpedoes, two Lewis guns, two depth charges, smoke boxes, twin engines, and twin shafts. The earlier 55′ boats were powered by twin 275-hp engines, but power in later boats varied between 375 and 450 hp per engine, delivering speeds of 34 to 40 knots. Typical details of a Thornycroft 55′ CMB were: 55′, 11′ beam, 6.1′ moulded depth, 3.2′ draft, maximum speed 40.4 knots, sustained speed 39 knots, twin 450-hp engines, 26,796 pounds displacement, 420-gallon fuel capacity, 200-nautical-mile range, and a crew of five men (two officers, two engine mechanics, one radio operator). These boats were able to make an amazing 35 knots in Sea State 4 (whitecapped waves of 4′ to 8′ with seas building under winds of 14 to 27 knots), but the heavy stresses involved made high demands on hull and crew.

The armament of the 55′ CMBs varied considerably. At the suggestion of the Admiralty's Anti-Submarine Department, some boats carried only one torpedo, and the saving in weight was distributed between additional Lewis guns and depth charges. Other boats were used simply as depth-charge carriers or for laying special mines which were originally designed for submarines. In 1917, 55′ CMBs numbered 14-18 were built, and 56 boats in all were completed up to the end of 1918. Sixteen additional boats did not enter service until 1919-1922.

As well as the first 40′ CMBs, numbered 1-13, built in 1916, an improved 38-knot 40-footer with a 350-hp Thornycroft engine was built in 1917-1918 and armed with an additional Lewis gun. There were 22 of these boats completed before the end of the war, and four more thereafter. Altogether, 91 CMBs were completed in Britain during the war, and another 25 were commissioned between 1919 and 1922.

The greatest secrecy was maintained throughout the design, building, and training operations of the CMBs, as their success would depend very much on the enemy's ignorance of their existence. The security was obviously successful, as the first pictures and printed confirmation of what Motorboat Magazine called "the fighting hydroplanes of the British Navy" did not appear in the United States until May of 1919.

As a training base, the South Eastern Railway Company pier at Queensborough had been decided upon, and those officers who volunteered for service on the first 40′ boats lived for some time on the pier. Very few people knew what these little boats were for, and their running for training purposes was carried out almost entirely at night. It was decided that the crew would consist of two officers and a motor mechanic, and,with a view towards everyone being thoroughly conversant with the all-important engines, the whole crew spent a month or more at the Basingstoke Works seeing them built and tested.

Very few mechanics with a knowledge of engines of 275 hp and of more or less the airplane type were available in England generally, and there certainly were none among the artificer branch of the Royal Navy.

During the attack, one of the CMB officers swept so close to fire his torpedo that the blast from one of the destroyers' 4.1″ guns blew his cap off without damage to his boat or injury to himself.

Not only had the officers to get proficient at handling their boats and firing their torpedoes under conditions of great strain at speeds well over 30 knots, but a staff of mechanics had to be trained to look after and maintain the machinery. However, after the few months practice, which they all had together, these crews were worked up to such an efficient stage that it would not have been possible for the boats and engines to have been running better. The captains of the different boats knew their brother officers' methods of handling and maneuvering so well that they were able to perform the most complicated group operations at night and at speed without difficulty.

The first war service was seen by the 40′ CMBs, four of which had been sent to Dunkirk in 1916. There was no prepared base, and the boats and their gear were berthed on a large steel barge in which the officers and crew lived throughout the winter. The winter was a very hard one, and great difficulty was experienced in keeping the engines and torpedoes from freezing up. However, the Dunkirk patrols were finally rewarded when, on the night of April 7, 1917, CMBs 4, 5, 6, and 9 sunk a German destroyer of 1147 tons off Ostend and damaged several others.

The Dunkirk boats compiled tens of thousands of miles of running in their patrol operations in the minefields before the entrances to Zeebrugge and Ostend. The Belgians who lived in these ports reported that the German naval authorities were in utter dread of them and never knew when to expect them. The German motor patrol boats, or PMBs, were of similar dimensions but never ventured out at night or when the CMBs were out as they were so much slower and less seaworthy. During their patrols up the coast, the CMBs were constantly fired at by shore batteries, and more than one was lost after receiving a direct hit.

The 55′ CMBs replaced the 40-footers in the Channel and on the Belgian-coast patrols in 1917. Owing to their larger dimensions, they were better sea boats and were more heavily armed. These boats patrolled the Belgian coast inside the sands and were able to keep a constant watch on Ostend and Zeebrugge. In one typical action, five German destroyers, returning from their dash through the Straits, encountered a small group of the British 55-footers, and one of them was torpedoed. During the attack, one of the CMB officers swept so close to fire his torpedo that the blast from one of the destroyers' 4.1″ guns blew his cap off without damage to his boat or injury to himself. The 40-footers, meanwhile, were still in the fray. For North Sea work, a new base was established not far from Harwich and residents there and in nearby Felixstowe became familiar with the sight of light cruisers putting out to sea with a couple of 40′ CMBs hanging from their davits.

The quickness with which the CMBs could work up to their top speed enabled them to get away successfully after attacks on warships. However, the greater speed of the airplane, as was expected, made it a formidable adversary when met with in daylight. In the summer of 1917, six boats were reported lost after a hostile airplane attack of great numbers. Four of these boats made their way to Holland after accounting for several of the attacking planes and using up all the ammunition for their Lewis guns. CMB crews often had to defend themselves against airplane attacks, and boats and men were hit on numerous occasions. In one particular North Sea action, after their boats had been riddled and most of the officers hit, Lieutenant Lewis—who was wounded himself—succeeded in keeping another officer afloat on a large fender for several hours and thus saving his life. These were gallant boats and men, a fleet of Davids against Goliaths.

The blocking action at Zeebrugge and Ostend has been much described as far as the larger vessels go, but it is not generally known what a leading role the CMBs played or that many of the officers who were given decorations in these actions were in charge of them. The strategic importance of closing up Zeebrugge and Ostend was of very great importance to the British. There nested the German destroyer flotillas which raided the narrow seas and kept the Dover Patrol busy most of the time. The chief weapon against the U-boat was the destroyer, and the presence of German vessels in the Belgian ports withdrew a large number of British destroyers from the anti-submarine campaign. Could Zeebrugge and Ostend be put out of action, the German naval front would be pushed back 300 miles to Emden, and Britain's East Coast ports would become the natural bases from which to deal with attacks by enemy surface craft on the Channel. A plan had been under consideration since November, 1917, and its purpose was to block the end of the Bruges Canal at Zeebrugge and the entrance of Ostend harbour.

Zeebrugge was not so much a port as the sea end of Bruges Canal, and in the canal the enemy found a perfect harbor. Its mouth was flanked by two short piers or seawalls, and a large mole had been built in a curve to the west of the channel. The mole was the vital defense of the harbor and had a normal garrison of a thousand men. It bristled with artillery and machine guns, and all the coast was studded with long-range artillery. The Ostend harbor defenses were less elaborate; it was also the mouth of a canal, but had no mole as a flank guard. The problem of the Admiralty in both cases was to sink ships inside the canals so that, aided by the silt of the tides, they should block the entrance. In view of the strong defenses, it seemed a desperate adventure.

In the action at Zeebrugge, the CMBs were responsible for making covering smoke, which they did by the employment of chlor-sulphonic acid in their exhausts (this operation being carried out ahead of the blocking vessels), and to mark certain positions with flares to indicate turning points for the blocking ships. Two of them entered the harbor in the early stages of the operation to torpedo a vessel alongside the mole,

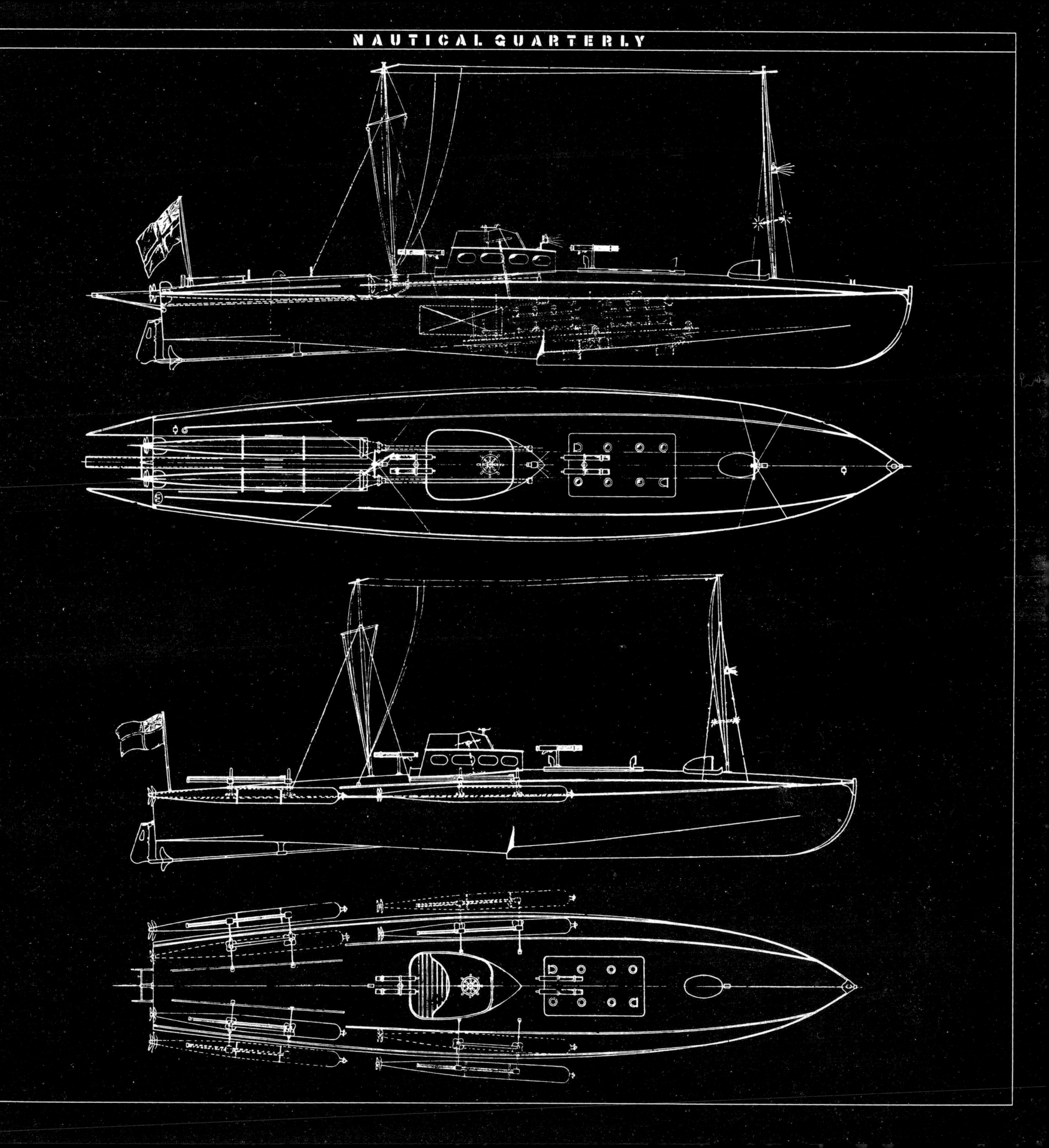

Thornycroft CMBs are seen in action on these pages, and the 55′ boat is seen in two versions on page 107 in plan form. The boats above and below are the 55-footer, and a 40-footer is shown on page 103 with a Thames Barge in the background. They were fast, dashing, deadly boats, as this article by Dan Wilkins and the short story by William Faulkner we are pleased to publish on following pages make clear.

Poor weather conditions and cold were very wearing on the crews, but they succeeded in causing the surrender of a number of vessels without actually torpedoing any of them.

while others were fitted with Stokes trench mortars to throw bombs over the mole to the airplane sheds.

In the second action at Ostend, two CMBs were detailed to torpedo the ends of the piers to put the guns on them out of action. Others went in ahead of the blocking ships to make smoke and to fire Very flares to indicate the exact position of the entrance. These little boats, as may well be imagined, were officered and manned by young men who gave no thought of tomorrow. They were accustomed to hurtling on in point blank range of the guns, and on the night of April 22-23, 1918, they again proved their value. It is a remarkable fact that, with one exception, all of the CMBs which took part in these blocking actions succeeded in getting away—although they were, in many cases, very battered and had many officers and men wounded.

Other actions by the CMBs included minelaying (their shallow draft enabling them to pass over enemy minefields, and their high speed enabling them to sweep into enemy waters unexpectedly), anti-submarine duty, air/sea rescue, merchant marine escort, etc. It is not possible in this brief article to give an account of all the operations and activities of these boats during W.W.I or of all the gallant deeds of their officers and crews. A long list of CMB officers who received the DSO, DSM, and other honors gives the best indication of the high opinion the Admiralty held of the role they played in the naval war. The Royal Navy lost a total of 15 CMBs due to war action—nine 40′ and six 55′ boats. A much greater number of officers and men were killed or badly wounded, with a casualty percentage comparable to that of the Air Service.

After the Armistice, it seemed that the work of the CMBs was finished. The advance base at Dunkirk was closed, and the boats and gear returned to Dover. Most of the operators were appointed away to big ships and the temporary officers and men were demobilized, the boats both at Dover and at other bases being left with care-and-maintenance parties. Before the Armistice, the cruiser *Diamond,* which had been fitted out as a carrying vessel for the CMBs, and six 40′ boats had been sent to the eastern Mediterranean, but an opportunity did not occur to employ them there. With the opening of the Dardanelles, it was decided to send these boats to Batoum and then put them on rail and transfer them to the Caspian Sea to augment the naval forces of the White Russians against the Bolsheviks. In addition to these boats, six others made an adventurous 600-mile railway journey from Batoum to the Black Sea, during which the CMB officers had to work the train themselves. At the time of the journey, it was difficult to discover which of the Russians were friends and which were enemies; both sides were determined to appropriate the gear and stores belonging to the boats.

Two trading vessels on the Caspian Sea were fitted out as carrying vessels for the CMBs and were kept at sea in readiness for an attack on the Bolshevik fleet. Poor weather conditions and cold were very wearing on the crews, but they succeeded in causing the surrender of a number of vessels without actually torpedoing any of them. The effect of a depth charge explosion in their vicinity was sufficient indication of the power of the small attacking craft to force capitulation. The Caspian was finally cleared of all Bolshevik vessels, the British officers sent home, and the boats handed over to friendly Russians.

In the meantime, there was naval action on the Archangel front, and it was decided to send a fleet of 55′ CMBs there. It was considered that there would be no opportunity for them to use their torpedoes, but their high speed and shallow draft, along with their machine guns, would be very effective in the advance up the Dvina River. These boats were fitted with six Lewis guns and portable armor plate protection. They advanced up the river with H.M.S. *Hyderabad,* a special shallow-draft steamer built by the British during the war as a decoy ship for German submarines, and the intention was to join the White Russian forces at Kotlas. This was to have been the rendezvous for a combined advance on Petrograd, but all forces failed to reach Kotlas. Lack of transport, the shallowness of the river, and the number of mines laid by the Bolsheviks were the principal causes of the failure. The CMBs had no great opportunity to distinguish themselves on this expedition. A great deal of running was done, however, with the boats often being sent downriver to Archangel and back (a distance of 500 miles), and the motors worked for very long periods without overhaul, often two or three times the period thought to be their limits.

While the fighting on the Caspian and Archangel front was coming to an end, it was well known that the British still had a fleet somewhere in the Baltic and that a blockade was being maintained to prevent the Bolshevik fleet from coming out of Petrograd Bay. The first incident to attract public attention on this front was a report from Finland that the Russian cruiser *Oleg* had been sunk. It was first reported by the Bolsheviks that she had been mined, and later reports alleged that she had been torpedoed by a submarine. It was not revealed until later that she had been done in by Lieutenant Agar in one of the 40′ CMBs as she guarded the entrance to Kronstadt harbor. The attack was on Agar's own initiative and was carried out without support from any other vessels. A protective screen of four Bolshevik destroyers was maintained outside the *Oleg,* but the lone CMB struck at dawn and succeeded in evading the destroyers, torpedoing the *Oleg* at short range and sinking her immediately. Soon after Agar's success, it was decided to send out a flotilla of CMBs.

Most of the original CMB officers had been appointed to big ships and the motor mechanics demobilized. It was an easy matter for the Admiralty to reappoint the officers, but the mechanics had all been hostilities men. The builders were asked to find volunteers, and eight 55′ CMBs were quickly sent to join the First Light Cruiser Squadron at Biorko Sound.

A great success was achieved at Kronstadt harbor, but it was at a cost of four officers and three men killed, three officers and six men wounded and imprisoned, and three boats destroyed.

Due to the uncharted shallow water and minefields, it would have been impossible for large vessels or even destroyers to have made a successful attack on Kronstadt harbor, but it was thought that there was a good chance for the CMBs. Photographs taken from the air showed the position of the vessels and the harbor layout and, since the torpedoing of the *Oleg*, only one destroyer was left to guard the entrance. August 17, 1919, was chosen for the night of the attack. At about 2130 hours, the eight CMBs took off from H.M.S. *Vindictive* in Biorko Sound. The weather conditions were ideal, dark and calm, and they ran to the rendezvous at Inonemi Point at about 18 knots. On the way, Lieutenant Agar's boat and two following CMBs were lost by the remainder who, at the appointed time, proceeded at speed to the attack. The vessels passed between the two outlying batteries of the harbor soon after an aerial bombardment which had been timed to coincide with the CMB attack.

The engine of CMB 86-BD, Sublieutenant Howard in command, seized a big end and remained outside the batteries while the attack took place. CMB 72-A, Sublieutenant Bodley, had its torpedo-firing gear shot away and arrived in the harbor somewhat after the first three boats, which were CMB 79-A, Lieutenant Bremner, CMB 31-BD, Lieutenant McBean, and CMB 88-BD, Lieutenant Dayrell-Reed.

According to plan, CMB 79-A entered the harbor first and torpedoed the submarine depot ship *Pamiat Azov.* She was closely followed by CMB 31-BD and 88-BD. CMB 31-BD's duty was to torpedo the *Andrei Pervozvanni* and then to hug the southern arm of the harbor, which it did. As CMB 88-BD was coming through the entrance, Lieutenant Dayrell-Reed was shot through the head and his second in command, Lieutenant Steele, immediately took over and torpedoed the *Andre Pervozvanni* and the *Petropavlovsk*. At about this time, Lieutenant Agar and the three remaining boats arrived outside the harbor to find the attack commenced. CMB 24-A, Lieutenant Napier, fired a torpedo at the destroyer outside but was afterwards sunk himself. CMB 62-BD, Lieutenant Brade, entered the harbor after CMBs 88 and 31 had left, but met with disaster as soon as he got inside. He and Lieutenant Bremner in CMB 79-A succeeded in getting their disabled boats outside the harbor, where Bremner blew up his boat. Brade then fired a torpedo at a destroyer leader and was sunk by gunfire. The only survivors of the two boats were Lieutenant Bremner, wounded in eleven places, and two crew members.

CMB 72-A, which had been with the first three boats going between the batteries, took a bullet through a carburetor and could not enter the harbor to torpedo the dock gates as planned. Her commander, Lieutenant Bodley, fired at a Russian destroyer, but his firing gear had been shot through and the torpedo failed to run. CMBs 31-BD and 88-BD managed to get out of the harbor and return to base. CMB 72-A managed to tow CMB 86-BD back to Biorko. CMB 4, Lieutenant Agar, was outside the harbor waiting to torpedo any ship which came out or to render assistance to any boat which needed it. He remained outside the harbor for a considerable time after the surviving boats had gone back, but failed to account for CMBs 62-BD, 24-A, and 79-A. Before leaving the harbor, he fired and hit a military transport and then remained outside the batteries until daylight.

As the surviving boats escaped, the harbor batteries were fully prepared for them with searchlights on the water. Their men feared that there was little chance for them to get through, but one airman, who appreciated their position, flew down into the beams of light and climbed rapidly. The Russians behind the searchlights could not resist following him with their beams, and the boats sped through invisible to the gunners.

A great success was achieved at Kronstadt harbor, but it was at a cost of four officers and three men killed, three officers and six men wounded and imprisoned, and three boats destroyed. Few men who took part in this action could have hoped to come out alive. There were three of the original CMB officers in the Kronstadt attack; Lieutenant Dayrell-Reed, who had taken part in the first CMB action at Zeebrugge, lost his life. The importance which the Admiralty attached to the operation can be judged by their award of decorations to all of the men and officers who took part, including Victoria Crosses to two of them.

During the 1920s, most of the CMBs in British possession were paid off and sold to other countries, while a few served out their time in the Royal Navy. Three 55′ CMBs were sold to the U.S. Navy and were given to the U.S. Coast Guard, which used them against liquor smugglers during the years of Prohibition.

It is revealing to compare the performance and structure of the 60-year-old CMBs to that of today's high-speed offshore raceboats. The following table lists the pertinent parameters of three such boats along with those of the CMBs.

The first thing to note is the respective structural weights. The 40′ CMB is somewhat lighter than the modern fiberglass hulls despite the fact that it had to carry a larger non-structural payload. Its hull of laminated American elm has a 15% higher strength/weight ratio than a typical E-type 'glass/resin lamination. Of course, no direct comparison can be made of the relative strengths of the various hulls, but there is no record of any structural failures in the CMBs despite the fact that they were pushed to the extreme limits of endurance in a war environment.

They were, of course, uncomfortable boats indeed, and only vigorous young men could stand the strains of high-speed operation at sea for any length of time. One 55′ CMB returned to base after a collision with its bow literally ripped off from deck to keel. During the Ostend attack, a launched torpedo failed and fired close under the stern of one of the boats, which was lifted a good many feet in the air. The after part of the hull was permanently deformed but was in no way fractured. After repairs to

"... the successes which have been obtained by them are due to the British Navy officers and men concerned, and without their skill and endurance the boats would have done nothing."

several engine connections, the boat was back in service. It is unlikely that the strength of Thornycroft's unique continuous-frame monocoque structure of laminated wood is surpassed by any but the most exotic structures and materials of today.

The second item of interest is the "K" Factor, a speed/efficiency measurement. The CMBs, for a given power and displacement, were "faster" than today's high-performance deep-vee hulls. Their actual top speeds were not higher because the CMBs did not have the light, powerful engines of today's boats. But if we were to install modern high-performance V8s in a 40′ CMB (and allow for the slight additional weights of multiple engines),we could predict speeds of 58 knots with twin 370s, 68 knots with three 370s, and 70 knots with twin 525s. This is 15% to 32% faster than modern boats with the same engines and similar displacements.

One must not be misled by this comparison, however, as hydroplanes will generally be more speed efficient than deep-vee monohulls. The deep-vees will generally have greater seakeeping ability than any hull with flatter sections. There is no way of knowing if a CMB could maintain comparable speed with a modern deep-vee in very rough offshore conditions. However, we do know that these boats performed at very respectable speeds in very rough conditions, and we may guess that they were an excellent balance between the speed efficiency of a hydroplane and the seakeeping ability of a deep-vee. The high efficiency of a 40′ Thornycroft CMB, with only one 250-hp engine, enabled it to carry a load of 15 people at more than 30 knots in Sea State 2-3. This high speed on low horsepower gave the CMBs relative economy in fuel consumption and thus a greater range at speed.

The CMBs proved their worth over and over again, and the data presented here would seem to argue strongly for a hull type of the deep-vee stepped form. However, the remarkable thing is that, in W.W.II and in the 40 years since, hydroplanes have not been used by any of the world's navies. The speed efficiency of the CMBs was not approached by any W.W.II boats, including the famed PT boats which had "K" Factors of only 109.

After the gallant deeds of his boats in W.W.I, John Thornycroft wrote: "While the designers and builders alike take pride in their production, they are all agreed that, however good the boats may be, the successes which have been obtained by them are due to the British Navy officers and men concerned, and without their skill and endurance the boats would have done nothing."

Parameter	36′ Cigarette	377 KAAMA Scarab	402 Formula	40′ CMB	55′ CMB
LOA	35′ 8″	37′ 7″	40′ 2″	40′	55′
Beam	9′ 3″	8′	9′ 4″	8′ 6″	11′
Displacement	11,200 lbs.	9,100 lbs.	9,000 lbs.	9,570 lbs.	26,800 lbs.
Power	3 x 370 hp.	2 x 525 hp.	2 x 370 hp.	1 x 375 hp.	2 x 450 hp.
Engine Weight	3,600 lbs.	2,400 lbs.	2,400 lbs.	2,090 lbs.	6,120 lbs.
Maximum Speed	57 knots	61 knots	43 knots	40 knots	40 knots
Structural Weight	5,420 lbs.	5,270 lbs.	4,900 lbs.	4,500 lbs.	11,000 lbs.
K Factor*	117	116	105	138	140

*The K Factor is an indication of the speed efficiency of a boat in an equation of the form:

$$\text{Speed} = K \frac{(\text{Horsepower})^{\text{exponent}}}{(\text{Displacement})^{\text{exponent}}}$$

The greater the K Factor, the faster a boat will be with all other factors equal.

(The author wishes to acknowledge the following sources for their particularly valuable contributions to the information in this article: *Short History of the Revival of the Small Torpedo Boat,* John I. Thornycroft & Co. Ltd., 1919; *CMB's, Their Design and Service During the War,* Sir J.E. Thornycroft, KBE, and Lieutenant Bremner, RN, D.S.O., 1925; *Fast Fighting Boats 1870-1945,* Harald Fock, 1973.)

TURN[A]

A marine with a bayoneted rifle passed Bogard onto the wharf and directed him to the boat. The wharf was empty, and he didn't even see the boat until he approached the edge of the wharf and looked directly down into it and upon the backs of two stooping men in greasy dungarees, who rose and glanced briefly at him and stooped again. □ It was about thirty feet long and about three feet wide. It was painted with gray-green camouflage. It was quarterdecked forward, with two blunt, raked exhaust stacks. "Good Lord," Bogard thought, "if all that deck is engine—" Just aft the deck was the control seat; he saw a big wheel, an instrument panel. Rising to a height of about a foot above the free-board, and running from the stern forward to where the deck began, and continuing on across the after edge of the deck and thence back down the other gunwale to the stern, was a solid screen, also camouflaged, which inclosed the boat save for the width of the stern, which was open. Facing the steersman's seat like an eye was a hole in the screen about eight inches in diameter. And looking down into the long, narrow, still, vicious shape, he saw a machine gun swiveled at the stern, and he looked at the low screen—including which the whole vessel did not sit much more than a yard above water level—with its single empty forward-staring eye, and he thought quietly: "It's steel. It's made of steel." And his face was quite sober, quite thoughtful, and he drew his trench coat about him and buttoned it, as though he were getting cold. □ He heard steps behind him and turned. But it was only an orderly from the aerodrome, accompanied by the marine with the rifle. The orderly was carrying a largish bundle wrapped in paper.

BY WILLIAM FAULKNER

ABOUT

THE ILLUSTRATION ABOVE IS REPRINTED FROM A 1932 NUMBER OF THE SATURDAY EVENING POST. IT WAS USED TO ILLUSTRATE THIS STORY BY WILLIAM FAULKNER, AND READERS NOW FAMILIAR WITH THE CMBs WILL NOTE HOW WONDERFULLY INACCURATE IT IS. THE BOAT IN THE ILLUSTRATION IS AN OPEN OUTBOARD OF ABOUT 20′ WITH A VERY SMALL MOTOR. THE HELMSMAN LOOKS TO BE WEARING A PITH HELMET.

"From Lieutenant McGinnis to the captain," the orderly said.

Bogard took the bundle. The orderly and the marine retreated. He opened the bundle. It contained some objects and a scrawled note. The objects were a new yellow silk sofa cushion and a Japanese parasol, obviously borrowed, and a comb and a roll of toilet paper. The note said:

Couldn't find a camera anywhere and Collier wouldn't let me have his mandolin. But maybe Ronnie can play on the comb.

MAC.

Bogard looked at the objects. But his face was still quite thoughtful, quite grave. He rewrapped the things and carried the bundle on up the wharf and dropped it quietly into the water.

As he returned toward the invisible boat he saw two men approaching. He recognized the boy at once—tall, slender, already talking, voluble, his head bent a little toward his shorter companion, who plodded along beside him, hands in pockets, smoking a pipe. The boy still wore the pea-coat beneath a flapping oilskin, but in place of the rakish and casual cap he now wore an infantryman's soiled Balaclava helmet, with, floating behind him as though upon the sound of his voice, a curtainlike piece of cloth almost as long as a burnous.

"Hullo, there!" he cried, still a hundred yards away.

But it was the second man that Bogard was watching, thinking to himself that he had never in his life seen a more curious figure. There was something stolid about the very shape of his hunched shoulders, his slightly down-looking face. He was a head shorter than the other. His face was ruddy, too, but its mold was of a profound gravity that was almost dour. It was the face of a man of twenty who has been for a year trying, even while asleep, to look twenty-one. He wore a high-necked sweater and dungaree slacks; above this a leather jacket; and above this a soiled naval officer's warmer that reached almost to his heels and which had one shoulder strap missing and not one remaining button at all. On his head was a plaid fore-and-aft deer stalker's cap, tied on by a narrow scarf brought across and down, hiding his ears, and then wrapped once about his throat and knotted with a hangman's noose beneath his left ear. It was unbelievably soiled, and with his hands elbow-deep in his pockets and his hunched shoulders and his bent head, he looked like someone's grandmother hung, say, for a witch. Clamped upside down between his teeth was a short brier pipe.

"Here he is!" the boy cried. "This is Ronnie. Captain Bogard."

"How are you?" Bogard said. He extended his hand. The other said no word, but his hand came forth, limp. It was quite cold, but it was hard, calloused. But he said no word; he just glanced briefly at Bogard and then away. But in that instant Bogard caught something in the look, something strange—a flicker; a kind of covert and curious respect, something like a boy of fifteen looking at a circus trapezist.

But he said no word. He ducked on; Bogard watched him drop from sight over the wharf edge as though he had jumped feet first into the sea. He remarked now that the engines in the invisible boat were running.

"We might get aboard too," the boy said... He descended first, the two men in the boat rising and saluting. Ronnie had disappeared, save for his backside, which now filled a small hatch leading forward beneath the deck. Bogard descended gingerly.

"Good Lord," he said. "Do you have to climb up and down this every day?"

"Frightful, isn't it?" the other said, in his happy voice. "But you know yourself. Try to run a war with makeshifts, then wonder why it takes so long." The narrow hull slid and surged, even with Bogard's added weight. "Sits right on top, you see," the boy said. "Would float on a lawn, in a heavy dew. Goes right over them like a bit of paper."

"It does?" Bogard said.

"Oh, absolutely. That's why, you see." Bogard didn't see, but he was too busy letting himself gingerly down to a sitting posture. There were no thwarts; no seats save a long, thick, cylindrical ridge which ran along the bottom of the boat from the driver's seat to the stern. Ronnie had backed into sight. He now sat behind the wheel, bent over the instrument panel. But when he glanced back over his shoulder he did not speak. His face was merely interrogatory. Across his face there was now a long smudge of grease. The boy's face was empty, too, now.

"Right," he said. He looked forward, where one of the seamen had gone. "Ready forward?" he said.

"Aye, sir," the seaman said.

The other seaman was at the stern line. "Ready aft?"

"Aye, sir."

"Cast off." The boat sheered away, purring, a boiling of water under the stern. The boy looked down at Bogard. "Silly business. Do it shipshape, though. Can't tell when silly fourstriper—" His face changed again, immediate, solicitous. "I say. Will you be warm? I never thought to fetch—"

"I'll be all right," Bogard said. But the other was already taking off his oilskin. "No, no," Bogard said. "I won't take it."

"You'll tell me if you get cold?"

"Yes. Sure." He was looking down at the cylinder on which he sat. It was a half cylinder—that is, like the hotwater tank to some Gargantuan stove, sliced down the middle and bolted, open side down, to the floor plates. It was twenty feet long and more than two feet thick. Its top rose as high as the gunwales and between it and the hull on either side was just room enough for a man to place his feet to walk.

"That's Muriel," the boy said.

"Muriel?"

"Yes. The one before that was Agatha. After my aunt. The first one Ronnie and I had was Alice in Wonderland. Ronnie and I were the White Rabbit. Jolly, eh?"

"Oh, you and Ronnie have had three, have you?"... He looked astern, and then he thought: "Good Lord! We must be going—traveling." He looked out now, broadside, and saw the harbor line fleeing past, and he thought to himself that the boat was well-nigh moving at the speed at which the Handley-Page flew, left the ground. They were beginning to bound now, even in the sheltered water, from one wave crest to the next with a distinct shock. His hand still rested on the cylinder on which he sat. He looked down at it again, following it from where it seemed to emerge beneath Ronnie's seat, to where it beveled into the stern. "It's the air in her, I suppose," he said.

"The what?" the boy said.

"The air. Stored up in her. That makes the boat ride high."

"Oh, yes. I dare say. Very likely. I hadn't thought about it." He came forward, his burnous whipping in the wind, and sat down beside Bogard. Their heads were below the top of the screen.

Astern the harbor fled, diminishing, sinking into the sea. The boat had begun to lift now, swooping forward and down, shocking almost stationary for a moment, then lifting and swooping again; a gout of spray came aboard over the bows like a flung shovelful of shot. "I wish you'd take this coat," the boy said.

Bogard didn't answer. He looked around at the bright face. "We're outside, aren't we?" he said quietly.

"Yes.... Do take it, won't you?"

"Thanks, no. I'll be all right. We won't be long, anyway, I guess."

"No. We'll turn soon. It won't be so bad then."

"Yes. I'll be all right when we turn." Then they did turn. The motion became easier. That is, the boat didn't bang head-on, shuddering, into the swells. They came up beneath now, and the boat fled with increased speed, with a long, sickening, yawing motion, first to one side and then the other. But it fled on, and Bogard looked astern with that same soberness with which he had first looked down into the boat. "We're going east now," he said.

"With just a spot of north," the boy said. "Makes her ride a bit better, what?"

"Yes," Bogard said. Astern there was nothing now save empty sea and the delicate needlelike cant of the machine gun against the boiling and slewing wake, and the two seamen crouching quietly in the stern. "Yes. It's easier." Then he said: "How far do we go?"

The boy leaned closer. He moved closer. His voice was happy, confidential, proud, though lowered a little: "It's Ronnie's show. He thought of it. Not that I wouldn't have in time. Gratitude and all that. But he's the older, you see. Thinks fast. Courtesy, *noblesse oblige*—all that. Thought of it soon as I told him this morning. I said, 'Oh, I say. I've been there. I've seen it'; and he said, 'Not flying'; and I said, 'Strewth'; and he said 'How far? No lying now'; and I said, 'Oh, far. Tremendous. Gone all night'; and he said, 'Flying all night. That must have been to Berlin'; and I said, 'I don't know. I dare say'; and he thought. I could see him thinking. Because he is the older, you see. More experience in courtesy, right thing. And he said, 'Berlin. No fun to that chap, dashing out and back with us.' And he thought and I waited, and I said, 'But we can't take him to Berlin. Too far. Don't know the way, either'; and he said—fast, like a shot—said, 'But there's Kiel'; and I knew—"

"What?" Bogard said. Without moving, his whole body sprang. "Kiel? In this?"

"Absolutely. Ronnie thought of it. Smart, even if he is a stickler. Said at once, 'Zeebrugge no show at all for that chap. Must do best we can for him. Berlin,' Ronnie said. 'My Gad! Berlin.' "

"Listen," Bogard said. He had turned now, facing the other, his face quite grave. "What is this boat for?"

"For?"

"What does it do?" Then, knowing beforehand the answer to his own question, he said, putting his hand on the cylinder: "What is this in here? A torpedo, isn't it?"

"I thought you knew," the boy said.

"No," Bogard said. "I didn't know." His voice seemed to reach him from a distance, dry, cricketlike: "How do you fire it?"

"Fire it?"

"How do you get it out of the boat? When that hatch was open a while ago I could see the engines. They were right in front of the end of this tube."

"Oh," the boy said. "You pull a gadget there and the torpedo drops out astern. As soon as the screw touches the water it begins to turn, and then the torpedo is ready, loaded. Then all you have to do is turn the boat quickly and the torpedo goes on."

"You mean—" Bogard said. After a moment his voice obeyed him again. "You mean you aim the torpedo with the boat and release it and it starts moving, and you turn the boat out of the way and the torpedo passes through the same water that the boat just vacated?"

"Knew you'd catch on," the boy said. "Told Ronnie so. Airman. Tamer than yours, though. But can't be helped. Best we can do, just on water. But knew you'd catch on."

"Listen," Bogard said. His voice sounded to him quite calm. The boat fled on, yawing over the swells. He sat quite motionless. It seemed to him that he could hear himself talking to himself: "Go on. Ask him. Ask him what? Ask him how close to the ship do you have to be before you fire.... Listen," he said, in that calm voice. "Now, you tell Ronnie, you see. You just tell him—just say—" He could feel his voice ratting off on him again, so he stopped it. He sat quite motionless, waiting for it to come back; the boy leaning now, looking at his face. Again the boy's voice was solicitous:

"I say. You're not feeling well. These confounded shallow boats."

"It's not that," Bogard said. "I just—Do your orders say Kiel?"

"Oh, no. They let Ronnie say. Just so we bring the boat back. This is for you. Gratitude. Ronnie's idea. Tame, after flying. But if you'd rather, eh?"

"Yes, some place closer. You see, I—"

"Quite. I see. No vacations in wartime. I'll tell Ronnie." He went forward. Bogard did not move. The boat fled in long, slewing swoops. Bogard looked quietly astern, at the scudding sea, the sky.

"My God!" he thought. "Can you beat it? Can you beat it?"

The boy came back; Bogard turned to him a face the color of dirty paper. "All right now," the boy said. "Not Kiel. Nearer place, hunting probably just as good. Ronnie says he knows you will understand." He was tugging at his pocket. He brought out a bottle. "Here. Haven't forgot last night. Do the same for you. Good for the stomach, eh?"

Bogard drank, gulping—a big one. He extended the bottle, but the boy refused. "Never touch it on duty," he said. "Not like you chaps. Tame here."

The boat fled on. The sun was already down the west. But Bogard had lost all count of time, of distance. Ahead he could see white seas through the round eye opposite Ronnie's face, and Ronnie's hand on the wheel and the granitelike jut of his profiled jaw and the dead upside-down pipe. The boat fled on.

Then the boy leaned and touched his shoulder. He half rose. The boy was pointing. The sun was reddish; against it, outside them and about two miles away, a vessel—a trawler, it looked like—at anchor swung a tall mast.

"Lightship!" the boy shouted. "Theirs." Ahead Bogard could see a low, flat mole—the entrance to a harbor. "Channel!" the boy shouted. He swept his arm in both directions. "Mines!" His voice swept back on the wind. "Place filthy with them. All sides. Beneath us too. Lark, eh?"

Against the mole a fair surf was beating. Running before the seas now, the boat seemed to leap from one roller to the next; in the intervals while the screw was in the air the engine seemed to be trying to tear itself out by the roots. But it did not slow; when it passed the end of the mole the boat seemed to be standing almost erect on its rudder, like a sailfish. The mole was a mile away. From the end of it little faint lights began to flicker like fireflies. The boy leaned. "Down," he said. "Machine guns. Might stop a stray."

"What do I do?" Bogard shouted. "What can I do?"

"Stout fellow! Give them hell, what? Knew you'd like it!"

Crouching, Bogard looked up at the boy, his face wild. "I can handle the machine gun!"

"No need," the boy shouted back. "Give them first innings. Sporting. Visitors, eh?" He was looking forward. "There she is. See?" They were in the harbor now, the basin opening before them. Anchored in the channel was a big freighter. Painted midships of the hull was a huge Argentine flag. "Must get back to stations!" the boy shouted down to him. Then at that moment Ronnie spoke for the first time. The boat was hurtling along now in smoother water. Its speed did not slacken and Ronnie did not turn his head when he spoke. He just swung his jutting jaw and the clamped cold pipe a little, and said from the side of his mouth a single word:

"Beaver."

The boy, stooped over what he had called his gadget, jerked up, his expression astonished and outraged. Bogard also looked forward and saw Ronnie's arm pointing to starboard. It was a light cruiser at anchor a mile away. She had basket masts, and as he looked a gun flashed from her after turret. "Oh, damn!" the boy cried. "Oh, you putt! Oh, confound you, Ronnie! Now I'm three down!" But he had already stooped again over his gadget, his face bright and empty and alert again; not sober; just calm, waiting. Again Bogard looked forward and felt the boat pivot on its rudder and head directly for the freighter at terrific speed, Ronnie now with one hand on the wheel and the other lifted and extended at the height of his head.

But it seemed to Bogard that the hand would never drop. He crouched, not sitting, watching with a kind of quiet horror the painted flag increase like a moving picture of a locomotive taken from between the rails. Again the gun crashed from the cruiser behind them, and the freighter fired point-blank at them from its poop. Bogard heard neither shot.

"Man, man!" he shouted. "For God's sake!"

Ronnie's hand dropped. Again the boat spun on its rudder. Bogard saw the bow rise, pivoting; he expected the hull to slam broadside on into the ship. But it didn't. It shot off on a long tangent. He was waiting for it to make a wide sweep, heading seaward, putting the freighter astern, and he thought of the cruiser again. "Get a broadside, this time, once we clear the freighter," he thought. Then he remembered the freighter, the torpedo, and he looked back toward the freighter to watch the torpedo strike, and saw to his horror that the boat was now bearing down on the freighter again, in a skidding turn. Like a man in a dream, he watched himself rush down upon the ship and shoot past under her counter, still skidding, close enough to see the faces on her decks. "They missed and they are going to run down the torpedo and catch it and shoot it again," he thought idiotically.

So the boy had to touch his shoulder before he knew he was behind him. The boy's voice was quite calm: "Under Ronnie's seat there. A bit of a crank handle. If you'll just hand it to me—"

He found the crank. He passed it back; he was thinking dreamily: "Mac would say they had a telephone on board." But he didn't look at once to see what the boy was doing with it, for in that still and peaceful horror he was watching Ronnie, the cold pipe rigid in his jaw, hurling the boat at top speed round and round the freighter, so near that he could see the rivets in the plates. Then he looked aft, his face wild, importunate, and he saw what the boy was doing with the crank. He had fitted it into what was obviously a small windlass low on one flank of the tube near the head. He glanced up and saw Bogard's face. "Didn't go that time!" he shouted cheerfully.

"Go?" Bogard shouted. "It didn't—The torpedo—"

The boy and one of the seamen were quite busy, stooping over the windlass and the tube. "No. Clumsy. Always happening. Should think clever chaps like engineers—Happens, though. Draw her in and try her again."

"But the nose, the cap!" Bogard shouted. "It's still in the tube, isn't it? It's all right, isn't it?"

"Absolutely. But it's working now. Loaded. Screw's started turning. Get it back and drop it clear. If we should stop or slow up it would overtake us. Drive back into the tube. Bingo! What?"

Bogard was on his feet now, turned, braced to the terrific merry-go-round of the boat. High above them the freighter seemed to be spinning on her heel like a trick picture in the movies. "Let me have that winch!" he cried.

"Steady!" the boy said. "Mustn't draw her back too fast. Jam her into the head of the tube ourselves. Same bingo! Best let us. Every cobbler to his last, what?"

"Oh, quite," Bogard said. "Oh, absolutely." It was like someone else was using his mouth. He leaned, braced, his hands on the cold tube, beside the others. He was hot inside, but his outside was cold. He could feel all his flesh jerking with cold as he watched the blunt, grained hand of the seaman turning the windlass in short, easy, inch-long arcs, while at the head of the tube the boy bent, tapping the cylinder with a spanner, lightly, his head turned with listening delicate and deliberate as a watchmaker. The boat rushed on in those furious, slewing turns. Bogard saw a long, drooping thread loop down from somebody's mouth, between his hand, and he found that the thread came from his own mouth.

He didn't hear the boy speak, nor notice when he stood up. He just felt the boat straighten out, flinging him to his knees beside the tube. The seaman had gone back to the stern and the boy stooped again over his gadget. Bogard knelt now, quite sick. He did not feel the boat when it swung again, nor hear the gun from the cruiser which had not dared to fire and the freighter which had not been able to fire, firing again. He did not feel anything at all when he saw the huge, painted flag directly ahead and increasing with locomotive speed, and Ronnie's lifted hand drop. But this time he knew that the torpedo was gone; in pivoting and spinning this time the whole boat seemed to leave the water; he saw the bow of the boat shoot skyward like the nose of a pursuit ship going into a wingover. Then his outraged stomach denied him. He saw neither the geyser nor heard the detonation as he sprawled over the tube. He felt only a hand grasp him by the slack of his coat, and the voice of one of the seamen: "Steady all, sir. I've got you."

A voice roused him, a hand. He was half sitting in the narrow starboard runway, half lying across the tube. He had been there for quite a while; quite a while ago he had felt someone spread a garment over him. But he had not raised his head. "I'm all right." he had said. "You keep it."

"Don't need it," the boy said. "Going home now."

"I'm sorry I—" Bogard said.

"Quite. Confounded shallow boats. Turn any stomach until you get used to them. Ronnie and I both, at first. Each time. You wouldn't believe it. Believe human stomach hold so much. Here." It was the bottle. "Good drink. Take enormous one. Good for stomach."

Bogard drank. Soon he did feel better, warmer. When the hand touched him later, he found that he had been asleep.

It was the boy again. The pea-coat was too small for him; shrunken, perhaps. Below the cuffs his long, slender, girl's wrists were blue with cold. Then Bogard realized what the garment was that had been laid over him...

Bogard rose and sat on the tube. The entrance to the harbor was just ahead; the boat had slowed a little. It was just dusk. He said quietly: "Does this often happen?" The boy looked at him. Bogard touched the tube. "This. Failing to go out."

"Oh, yes. Why they put the windlass on them. That was later. Made first boat; whole thing blew up one day. So put on windlass."

"But it happens sometimes, even now? I mean, sometimes they blow up, even with the windlass?"

"Well, can't say, of course. Boats go out. Not come back. Possible. Not ever know, of course. Not heard of one captured yet, though. Possible. Not to us, though. Not yet."

"Yes," Bogard said. "Yes." They entered the harbor, the boat moving still fast, but throttled now and smooth, across the dusk-filled basin... The boat drifted in; the seaman had again crawled forward onto the deck. Ronnie spoke for the third and last time. "Right," he said.

"I want," Bogard said, "a case of Scotch. The best we've got. And fix it up good. It's to go to town. And I want a responsible man to deliver it." The responsible man came. "This is for a child," Bogard said, indicating the package. "You'll find him in the Street of the Twelve Hours, somewhere near the Café Twelve Hours. He'll be in the gutter. You'll know him. A child about six feet long. Any English M. P. will show him to you. If he is asleep, don't wake him. Just sit there and wait until he wakes up. Then give him this. Tell him it is from Captain Bogard."

About a month later a copy of the English Gazette which had strayed onto an American aerodrome carried the following item in the casualty lists:

Missing: Torpedo Boat XOOI. Midshipmen R. Boyce Smith and L. C. W. Hope, R. N. R., Boatswain's Mate Burt and Able Seaman Reeves. Channel Fleet, Light Torpedo Division. Failed to return from coast patrol duty.

Shortly after that the American Air Service headquarters also issued a bulletin:

For extraordinary valor over and beyond the routine of duty, Captain H. S. Bogard, with his crew, composed of Second Lieutenant Darrel McGinnis and Aviation Gunners Watts and Harper, on a daylight raid and without scout protection, destroyed with bombs an ammunition depot several miles behind the enemy's lines. From here, beset by enemy aircraft in superior numbers, these men proceeded with what bombs remained to the enemy's corps headquarters at Blank and partially demolished this château, and then returned safely without loss of a man.

And regarding which exploit, it might have added, had it failed and had Captain Bogard come out of it alive, he would have been immediately and thoroughly court-martialed.

Carrying his remaining two bombs, he had dived the Handley-Page at the château where the generals sat at lunch, until McGinnis, at the toggles below him, began to shout at him, before he ever signaled. He didn't signal until he could discern separately the slate tiles of the roof. Then his hand dropped and he zoomed, and he held the aeroplane so, in its wild snarl, his lips parted, his breath hissing, thinking: "God! God! If they were all there—all the generals, the admirals, the presidents and the kings—theirs, ours—all of them."

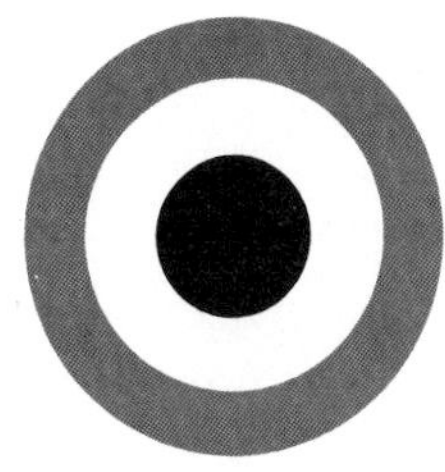

Editor's note: "Turnabout" is a two-part story by William Faulkner, one of a group of World War I stories Faulkner wrote after his own service as a pilot in the war. In the first part of "Turnabout," Captain Bogard, the proprietor of a Handley-Page bomber, takes the two young CMB officers on a bombing run over Germany. In this second part, they reciprocate with a wild torpedo run into Zeebrugge. The boat in this story is a 40′ CMB of laminated elm, not a 30-footer of steel as mistakenly described here.

Copyright © 1932, and renewed in 1960 by the Curtis Publishing Co. Reprinted from *Collected Stories of William Faulkner,* by William Faulkner, by permission of Random House, Inc.

CORRESPONDENCE

Dear Editor:

What a delightful surprise to receive the copy of Nautical Quarterly 13. The beautiful photographs and fascinating copy succeeded in stirring interest in even a landlubber such as I. I've shared the publication with co-workers at the Gallery and it's been getting rave reviews. Thanks.

Patricia Schrepel
National Gallery of Art
Washington, D.C.

Dear Editor:

Please be advised that I'm reinstating my subscription. I had earlier canceled but I was so impressed with your new hardbound issue that I want to continue. Enclosed is my check. Thank you for a lovely magazine.

Kevin Jones
Staten Island, New York

Dear Editor:

You have prepared the most beautiful set of "books" on boating, the oceans, and their history, that it has ever been my pleasure to read. I was first introduced to Nautical Quarterly by my father who, upon leaving Alaska, "willed" me the first five volumes. I was hooked. Thank you for a fantastic publication. I wish you many years of success.

Randall Jacobs
Anchorage, Alaska

Dear Editor:

Nautical Quarterly 13 was my introduction to your fine publication. I was impressed with all the articles (I thought the article on the Hooligan Navy was well done), as well as the presentation and quality of the whole book. I hope it has a long life.

Douglas S. Turner
Falmouth Marine Railway, Inc.
Falmouth, Massachusetts

CORRESPONDENCE

Dear Editor:

Reference to our company's FORMICA® trademark appeared in Nautical Quarterly 13; while we appreciate your reference to FORMICA®, such reference was improper in that the specific phrase used, "head done in formica," does not refer to "FORMICA" in the proper trademark context. Your article implies that FORMICA is a product name, the same as "tile," "wood," "ceramic," etc. This results from the fact that you fail to indicate that FORMICA is a brand name and fail to use a product name in association with it. The term "FORMICA" has been used as a trademark and tradename by our company since 1914. It is registered with the United States patent and trademark office for decorative plastic laminate and other fine products. I am sure you can appreciate our concern for our trademark in view of the enormous good will we have built up in it over a substantial period of time.

You may wish in your future articles to use just "laminate surfacing" or "plastic laminate." However, if you prefer to use our FORMICA trademark to identify laminate made by our company, we ask your cooperation by using it in the form "FORMICA® decorative laminate," or if you prefer, "FORMICA® laminate" (use of the "®" is optional). You will note that the trademark may appear either in all capital letters or with an initial capital letter.

In view of the importance of this matter to us, we look forward to receiving your assurance of cooperation. Thank you.

Stanley J. Silverberg
Trademark Attorney
Formica Corporation
Wayne, New Jersey

Editor's Note: The Formica Corporation has Nautical Quarterly's assurance of future cooperation.

Dear Editor:

I just received Nautical Quarterly 13, and the great part of it is reading about some really great people and their work. I was particularly pleased with the description and narration of Hank Hinckley and the apt way John Atkin describes the man and his work. I agree Hank has a powerful desire to know the basics. In 1974 Hank left a good position at the Hinckley Company to join me in my small machine shop in Southwest Harbor, Maine. Hank had a powerful desire to learn that phase of the boat business as that was the prime part of our business. In the course of almost a year, Hank became a darn good machinist and my good friend. Then on to Palmer Johnson with Mike Kelsey describing Shuff Willman as his right hand man. I remember Shuff, my old shipmate of *Gypsy* for a lot of years, as a great competitor. I sailed with him and against him when I owned the 44′ *Revelry,* built by Henry Hinckley. We won a few and lost quite a few more.

I also had the great pleasure and privilege to sail with Clayton Ewing on *Dyna* for a few years in a few Bermuda races and a trans-Atlantic. If you have anything planned to say about him, I wouldn't be surprised as he is a whole story in one guy.

I like Nautical Quarterly and look forward to the next one to see if you'll say a few more things about the great guys that hang around boats.

Norman (Nub) Sarns
Gainesville, Florida

Editor's Note: Twenty years ago when ski boots were made of leather and you even had to lace them up, NQ's managing editor, Michael Levitt, learned to ski at the northern Michigan resort Nub's Nob, once owned by Nub Sarns. With fondness he remembers skiing such runs as Revelry Bowl, the numerous photos of Great Lakes racing boats on the barroom wall, and the warmth and good cheer dispensed there. A small world.

Dear Editor:

I am here to thank you very much for your kind regards and the nice Nautical Quarterly books. I have, with great interest, read them and was very pleased because of the marvelous pictures. The one book I have kept for myself, and the other is placed in our library, so that we can get use of it in our work.

E. Grimstad
The Viking Ship Museum
Roskilde, Denmark

Dear Editor:

I have seen a copy of the autumn issue 1980 of your magazine in which the Viking ships are dealt with in an extremely fine way. Several of the objects illustrated in your magazine come from our collections. More than one-third of the objects of the Viking exhibition recently on show in New York came from our museum, also. I wish to congratulate you on the excellent publication.

Olov Isaksson, Director
Museum of National Antiquities
Stockholm, Sweden

Dear Editor:

You were so very kind to send me a copy of NQ11 in which you published pictures and an article on my late father's catboat *Frolic*. I know he enjoyed the day with your photographer when my brother put *Frolic* through her paces. I am just sorry he did not live to see the article. He would have been very proud.

When my three children were growing up, they all enjoyed our summer visits to the Cape and the many, many sails on *Frolic*. *Frolic* now belongs to my brother, sister and myself. We hope we can keep her in the family, but a wooden boat is so costly to maintain these days that we will have to see how it goes.

Louise Cies
Brookline, Massachusetts

Dear Editor:

After receiving Nautical Quarterly for one year, I was fairly satisfied with the overall publication, especially the photography and "behind the scenes" articles. However, after receiving NQ12 I'm disappointed. NQ12 contains page after page of superficial bull.... and the articles really have little to do with boating. Lately, you people have "missed the boat." You should concentrate on sailing, cruising, personal accounts of passages and so forth, instead of folklore and model boats.

Bill Cunningham
Forest Grove, Oregon

Editors Note: We are tempted from time to time to deal with subjects that are peripheral to the world of yachts and the people who design, build, and enjoy them. The essays on the Vikings and the model-yacht sailors in Central Park in NQ12, and our visit to the liveaboard barges of Paris in NQ13, along with the piece on sharks in NQ13, were those kinds of subjects. Perhaps the piece on the British Coastal Motor Boats in this issue—triumphs of powerboat technology but now 60 years gone—is another one. Response to "Viking Ships" has run about 50-50 pro and con; response to the model yachts has been nil; and response to the Paris liveaboards has run to a few letters in which readers said, in essence, "those are not boats; they're apartments." We appreciate letters like Bill Cunningham's; they are a check on our own fallible judgment. We wish more readers would write with comments pro and con on the contents of this magazine.

Dear Editor:

It is with great pleasure that I have taken the time and the opportunity to examine carefully and admire the presentation, the typography and the general layout of Nautical Quarterly. I am fascinated by the photography in general. The illustrator Etienne Delessert introduced me to the series and he, too, appreciates it. I would very much appreciate if you would send me one copy of each issue from one to ten so I can complete my collection.

Jean Genoud
Lausanne, Switzerland

Dear Editor:

After that last letter from Morgan, you're probably wondering about our sanity. We are, too. The fish-house was broken into a couple of times when we were away, and Morgan swears they were putting something in our drinking water. So we buoyed the wreck (pop-up buoy, timed to release at the end of October) and have moved back to the Exchange for the Summer.

Damn, it's great to be back! While we were on Crotch Island this winter we did a lot of reading and discovered the historic implications of this area. Seems the Sippewisset Marsh was once a center for the construction and testing of eel traps. Not the box type—those are worthless for all but the most elementary sets—but the diminishing circle type. These are traps that allow the eel to enter and then force him to circle down through a tubular funnel. By the time he gets to the bottom his body is so tightly coiled he can't get back out. The Sippewisset Eel Coil was patented in 1873 and eventually found use up and down the eastern seaboard. They are still used in some of the minor eel-fishing ports of eastern Maine, but those we saw are of aberrant form when compared to the originals. Morgan and I have a specimen at the Exchange, and we hope to test it when the eels start running, which should be any day now. In the meantime, we have been sorting through the culch pile at Lefty Grogan's bait shack at the head of the Marsh to find the locking mechanism for the trap. I know Westerfield has one in his collection but he won't even let us borrow it for a day so it can be reproduced down at Al's machine shop. RSW III is so tight his cheeks squeak when he walks.

Fred Brooks, Prop.
Wood Neck Marine Antiques Exchange
Sippewisset, Massachusetts

CREDITS

Cover: Jim Brown

1-17: Eric Poggenpohl
18-20: Mimi Dyer
24: Mimi Dyer
28: Mimi Dyer
32: David Cover
33: Chris Cunningham
35: Courtesy of Surfer Magazine
36 & 38: Courtesy of The Hobie Hotline
39: Lawrence F. Salerno
40: Courtesy of The Hobie Hotline
41-49: Chris Cunningham
50-57: Jim Brown
58-60: Joe Upton
65: Drawings by J. P. Hartog, N.A.
70: Drawings by Edwin Monk, N.A.
71: Roy Montgomery
73: Drawings by Nils Lucander, N.A.
74-77: Allan Weitz
77: Courtesy of CSY Yacht Corp.
78-91: Eric Schweikardt
92 & 93: Allan Weitz
94 & 95: Photos by Allan Weitz Drawings by Gerhard Richter
96-98: Photos by Mark Warner
98: Drawing courtesy of Grand Banks Yachts, Ltd.
101: Bill Farrell
103: W. P. Trotter Collection, England
107: Courtesy of John I. Thornycroft & Co., Ltd., London, England
108: W. P. Trotter Collection, England
113: Reprinted from The Saturday Evening Post, © 1932, The Curtis Publishing Company
118: B. Martin Pedersen
120: Beken of Cowes Ltd., Cowes, England

Pages 96 through 99 commissioned by Grand Banks Yachts Ltd. by arrangement with John Atkin, yacht designer and surveyor. No editorial changes in John Atkin's survey text were made by Grand Banks Yachts Ltd. or its agents.

Nautical Quarterly is printed by LaSalle Industries, New York.